MERLIN AND VIVIEN

MORGAN LE FAY CASTS AWAY THE SCABBARD

Witches
and Wizards

THE SUPERNATURAL SERIES

BOOK
ONE

Witches AND Wizards

LUCY CAVENDISH

ROCKPOOL
PUBLISHING

A Rockpool book
PO Box 252
Summer Hill
NSW 2130
Australia
www.rockpoolpublishing.com.au
http://www.facebook.com/RockpoolPublishing

First published in 2016

All images are sourced from flickr.
Exceptions are page 86 shutterstock and pages 17, 18 and 34 are from Lucy Cavendish.
Page 135 image is from Australscope.
Page 146 from Fairfax media.

National Library of Australia Cataloguing-in-Publication entry

Cavendish, Lucy, author.

Witches and wizards : astonishing real-life stories behind
    the occult's greatest legends, myths and
    mysteries / Lucy Cavendish.

9781925017441 (hardback)

Supernatural series.
Includes bibliographical references.

Witches—Anecdotes.
    Wizards—Anecdotes.
    Wizards in literature.
    Witches in literature.
    Witchcraft—Anecdotes.

133.4

Cover and internal design by Seymour Design
Typeset by TypeSkill
Edited by Katie Evans
Printed and bound in China
10 9 8 7 6 5 4 3 2

Contents

An Introduction to Witches and Wizards

By Lucy Cavendish

Gather round, friends, for within these pages there are tales to be told of Wizards conjuring the Grain, of Witches summoning spirits to heal and to harm. Shocking stories of advisors to Queens, of cunning-men and women on windswept hills, of half-mad mages calling on the Gods of ancient Egypt, their cauldrons, wands and Magick still all about us, every single day.

Be aware – this is no book of fantasy. The occult legends you will discover within its pages are real. These legends were once (and some still are) flesh and blood like you and like me. They lived and loved, suffered and triumphed, and they all worked Magick in their own particular and sometimes very peculiar way. Each of them is fascinating in their own right, but together they are the very stuff of legend, the truth behind the fantasies that filter through our lives.

I've been exploring these beings for a very long time now. History, and in particular Magickal people's lives, are something of an obsession for me. This book is the result of years of study, travel to some fairly obscure and sometimes bizarre locations, research in old libraries and within musty tomes, all in order to truly understand who these people were.

When I first began to learn about these amazing Magickal human beings, their passions, their glories and tragedies, and their powerful influence, I truly had no-one to share my discoveries with. I was an ordinary and slightly odd girl, who lived in the sunburned suburbs in Sydney, and no-one I knew was the least interested in what was so compelling to me – Magick, myth and mystery consumed me! In time, I became a practising Witch, and then a public one. My first training circle was back in 1987, and my first tarot deck, bought the same year, was the Crowley-Thoth deck, with its paintings by Lady Frieda Harris. I journeyed into Avalon, and travelled the path of Druidry and the Wizards, and with this training I grew more and more fascinated with the layers behind the Witches and Wizards of legend. As I walked the streets of Sydney I would think about Rosaleen Norton, the Witch of King's Cross, busking with her art on the pavements to make enough money for her canvases. Walking the labyrinth of esoteric bookstores in London's Covent Garden I would ponder the members of the Golden Dawn, and the infamous Aleister Crowley, and in the vast British Museum I would hunt out again and again the small cabinet containing the Magickal tools of

Doctor John Dee, the Elizabethan Wizard whose work is even more influential today than ever before.

Flawed as they were, I was encouraged by these incredible people and their disregard for convention in far more dangerous times than those in which I live. I found them an inspiration as I began to work publicly as a Witch and encountered the inevitable backlash, misunderstandings and petty prejudices that coming out of the broom closet can bring. And of course I learned there were a lot of people like me – people who were intrigued by and drawn to these occult legends.

Now, with the hyper-success of books such as the Harry Potter series and the adaptation of the *Lord of the Rings* into blockbuster movies, so many people are hungry for the truth behind these fantasies. And while they are fiction, they have at their heart true ancient Magick. Behind these countless books, poems, paintings, fantasy television series and blockbuster movies stands a remarkable group of real-life people.

You see, Magick is no fantasy, and nor are Witches and Wizards. You will discover through their stories that they are not only powerful, they are all too human at times. There is something endearing and touching about knowing that the greatest and most gifted Witches and Wizards struggle just as you and I do. We often assume that when people connect deeply to the Magick within and without, above and below, that they become somehow immune to all the lessons of ordinary living. But this is not true, not for the least, nor for the greatest of us. Their feuds, their love affairs, their addictions, their conflicts, their mistakes and their contradictions are within these pages, not to point fingers, but to see just how human we all are. Sometimes, for all its rewards, being a Witch or a Wizard makes human life even more challenging, sometimes even downright dangerous. For these legends, fitting in might have been the safer option, but it was never a real possibility given their Magickal natures. So they are inspirations to all of us who feel at times more than a little weird according to the dictates of the mainstream.

There are so many who deserve to have their tales told, and this book is in no way even close to a complete history. There are so many people who died during the Burning Times, who were imprisoned during the Salem Witch Trials, or hung upon hills like the witches of Pendle. So many of them have been overlooked, forgotten. So, alongside the stories of the renowned and infamous, I've included small personal stories. I've included them so that their lives can have at least a little of the respect they are due.

The late nineteenth and twentieth centuries saw flamboyant Witches and Wizards emerge, some who outright courted attention, and their vibrancy, daring and revolutionary spirits have blazed a trail we are all walking to this day. Perhaps they even changed the course of history.

Without the Magickal Battle of Britain, could the Nazis have succeeded? Without the members of the Golden Dawn Society, we may not have tarot cards and divination. Without John Dee, the Merlin of Mortlake, would there be so many people, today, attempting to talk with the Angels?

Please know it is not my intent for *Witches and Wizards* to be in any way an exhaustive academic work, or a satisfying biography of each person featured within. Instead, this book attempts to bring them back into a context that doesn't trivialize their reality. People like Aleister Crowley and Rosaleen Norton were never far away from tabloid sensation, but they are owed respect, consideration and recognition as agents of amazing social change. Others simply deserve to have their personal stories told, like nineteen-year-old Gobelin of Werzberg, Germany, caught up in the frenzy of the *Malleus Maleficarum*-inspired witch hunts, or Edward Kelley, charlatan or greatest channeler, or Doreen Valiente, the modern mother of Witchcraft.

My hope is that through connecting with these amazing souls and their stories you will be inspired to live your own life with a little more courage. To be a little more daring, a little less compliant to convention, and to realise that your struggles and challenges make you a hero, and that you are Magickal, and Magickal people do not always have it easy – but they nearly always have lives that are rich and meaningful.

I wish you wonderful reading and a blessed and Magickal life. For perhaps you too are one of these Witches and Wizards, and the world needs you, now, to take your place and do your part in this evolution of the human spirit.

With brightest blessings
Lucy Cavendish
Blood Moon, 2015

A Snake Came Crawling

Pre History – the Dark Ages

EFORE THERE was terror there was a truce between the ways of the Old Gods and the New … in the Dark Ages, there was light in the form of harmony, and the web of Wyrd was respected by all – even by Christian Kings.

A Wizard stands still in the field at dawn, his eyes fixed on the horizon, every sense anticipating the first rays of the sunrise, to choosing the perfect moment to begin the ancient ceremony. He murmurs incantations softly in the still air, each verse gathering power as the sun moves closer to the edge of the horizon. Four sods of earth stitched with seed lie at his feet, a beautifully carved plough rests in the field. With every moment his voice grows stronger, wilder, and before long the people gathered around can begin to discern what he is saying. And they long to hear – for he is speaking the old words over the land, the Magickal sounds that will bring the fields back to life, the prayers that will bring forth the grain and the vegetables, the fruits and the seeds that will provide every one of them with life throughout the season – and seasons – to come.

Every member of the tiny community has brought something to this immense ritual – the ritual known as AEcerbot, or the Remedy, to bring fruit to the fields. The Field Remedy charm is no fanciful thing, no dalliance with Magick. This is a twenty-four-hour process, which began at sundown the night before, and the Wizard has not worked alone. For the new Church's priest has worked and prayed over four sods of earth taken from the fields of the parishioners. He has soaked their roots in the poultice of honey and oil and milk and herb made by the Wise Women. He has prayed over the sods, and said a mass for them. He took four crucifixes and planted them into each sod within the Church, inscribing names of saints upon each cross. The Wizard does not like this change in the charm – for once the runes were written upon the sods, but for now they have agreed the saints must be asked for their blessing too, and it eases the priest's mind to know that the fields will be sown with the saints' blessings, as well as those of the earth mother, of Odin, of the Aelfer, or the elves.

In the darkness of the early morning, the villagers helped carry the sods to the fields, and now they stand gathered, along with their priest, watching their Wizard prepare …

And it is then the Magick begins. As the sun turns the sky to gold and coral, the Wizard raises his arms, faces the east, and turns deosil – sunwise – three times, his voice growing in power and emotion, imploring the sun to fill the earth with its energy.

Each of the sods is ceremonially planted within the field, and the plough is then sprinkled with a strange mixture of frankincense, salt, oil and fennel …

The cries are taken up by the villagers as the plough, now blessed, begins to break the earth.

Mother of Earth …
Earth, Mother of mortals
Erce, Erce, Erce, Erce

❧

This blessing of the land was a common ritual in Dark Ages Britain – a strange concoction, part Christian, part pagan, totally Magickal, that took weeks to prepare, a complete commitment by the priest and the people and a Wizard. It is typical of the syncretism of faith at a time when Wizards and Witches, cunning-men and Wise Women worked alongside the evolving Christian faith. (Cunning meant, in the old language, naturally clever – it did not have the connotation it has today, of being sly.) Whether Magick and miracle, both were woven into each other's worlds.

Between around 400AD and 1300, the Dark Ages allowed an evolution in religion. In Britain, the old Celtic ways had met and been melded to a degree with the practices of Rome, their gods meeting with the old ones, creating new, synthesized deities such as Sulis-Minerva of the sacred springs of Bath.

Then came the Saxons, with their runes, and Odin, with
Thor and Freya, and then came a new wave, the Christians,
with their Christ – 'Christ', said St Columba, one of the
founders of Celtic Christianity, 'is my Druid.' After them
came the Vikings, and a further Nordic influence wove its
way into the land. Thus Druids and priests, warriors, farmers,
Wise Women and the cunning-folk who practised the
Earth Magick found some way of getting along – and by
finding where their worlds were similar, peace was possible.
It was not perfect – there are laws we can trace forbidding
malevolent Witchcraft, but the punishment for Magickal
malpractice was to do penance for a year, or to eat bread
and water for a time. King Alfred, who reigned as King
of England (871–91) was a man who acknowledged the
Magickal practice of his forebears – the philosophy known
as Wyrd – but as *he* understood Wyrd – the energy and the
weaving of fate and will that created lives – it was something
brought about by God. He said, 'What we call Wyrd is really
the work of God about which he is busy every day.'

What is Wyrd?

Wyrd is an Anglo-Saxon word that describes a complex
Nordic philosophy of fate, energy and free will and how
all these factors played out when combined with the

will of the Gods. It is often described as a great web – multi-dimensional, vast, extending into infinity – and this energetic web includes our current lifetime, past lifetimes, and even, some say, our lifetimes to come. It is impossible to sum up Wyrd easily or neatly – it is vast and mysterious, and not simply understood, especially by those of us conditioned to have instant answers and fast food. Wyrd (the root of the modern word 'weird') is the combination of free will, and our own personal destiny, and the will of the Gods, and the fate of our environment and countries, our families and bloodlines. If we study the word closely, its root means 'that which has turned' or 'that which has become'. It's thus linked to the idea of vast synchronicities at play behind what seems to be the 'real' world.

Because Wyrd is a web and multi-dimensional, every single thing in the world, seen and unseen, is connected and can have influence, one on the other, in an infinite series of variations and patterns. Each strand of the web, when moved, will have ramifications elsewhere, so Wyrd speaks greatly to the Magickal truth that all Wizards and Witches know – that energetic choices have profound consequences.

Thus it is profoundly important when the Wizard or the Witch works Magick to understand and respect this reality – whenever a strand on the web of Wyrd is plucked, there will be reactions and consequences elsewhere. We need to know what we are working with, and why, to avoid potentially harmful consequences. It's a little like being a musician playing upon the harp – you can either create music which is transcendent and uplifting, or you can hit the wrong notes, sending out ripples of discord.

Doctor Brian Bates, author of *The Way of Wyrd*, based in part on the Lacnunga – a collection of writings and prayers (Remedies) – is one of the world's foremost authorities on Anglo-Saxon Wizardry and Magick. His work has re-established Wyrd as a spiritual force to be reckoned with in the modern world. And while our word 'weird' is the modern-day ancestor of Wyrd, in ancient times the word was respected, honoured and sacred. 'The original, archaic form meant in Anglo-Saxon "destiny", but also "power", or "magic" or "prophetic knowledge". "Wyrd" was still the "unexplainable", but the unexplainable was the sacred, the very grounding of existence, the force which underlay all of life.'

King Alfred was a deeply committed Christian, a Warrior-King who fought off Viking invasions, and a shrewd, religious diplomat who encouraged kindness and mercy. His influence was immense and resulted in more and more churches being built in the little villages. Priests were encouraged to work with the Wizards and Wise Women, and Vikings became farmers and citizens of Wessex. It was a cunning – in the best sense of the word – form of conversion; a stealthy, shrewd wisdom that created opportunities for Christianity. achieved not through violence and force, but through clever manipulation of existing belief systems that resulted in the Christianisation of Old Briton.

In the Britain of the Anglo-Saxons, faith was a synthesis of the Old Ways and the new, and while churches like the little one at the village now known as Alton Priors in Wiltshire were being built, they were also part of a wider system of belief that had flourished and evolved for years.

Take, for example, this charm – one of the most famous of syncretic faith, known as the Nine Herbs Charm. This fragment reveals so much about the Anglo-Saxon world and its ability to meld forms of belief that later centuries would tear apart.

A snake came crawling, it bit a man.
Then Woden took nine glory-twigs,
Smote the serpent so that it flew into nine parts.
There apple brought this pass against poison,
That she nevermore would enter her house.

This spell was used widely and it can found in the tenth century Anglo-Saxon manuscript, the Lacnunga. It was common for charms to make mention of Christ or one of the Old Gods. The Nine Herbs Charm mentions Odin – Woden – and Christ.

So, although many people today believe that there was never a time when Witches and Wizards and Priests and Church lived alongside each other, the truth is that they did. Although they skirmished and fought, there was a tolerance – sometimes almost envy – towards many Magickal practices within the early Church, which sought to bring people to Christianity though absorbing the pagan rituals and ways that were too loved, too revered to move on. Today you can see images of the Green Man in Westminster Abbey, runes in a Saxon churchyard, and yew trees in every Christian cemetery. Ostara, the Goddess, became Easter, Yule or the Winter solstice became Christ-mass, and Samhain became All Hallows Eve. Woden's day became Wednesday, Thor's day became Thursday, Freya's day became Friday – we live in a world still defined by Wyrd and the path of the Anglo-Saxon Wizards and Witches.

So now we can see how it was: until the early middle ages, folk magic and Witchcraft survived – and sometimes even thrived – alongside Christianity. It was officially disapproved of, certainly, and looked upon with suspicion and sometimes condemnation. But as is now clear, many of the Anglo-Saxons' folk charms made use of working with Old Gods and Goddesses, faerie and elf, Christian saints and Angels all within the one ritual. The Nine Herbs Charm casts out curses and illness by calling upon both Christ and Odin, and was used to heal Christian and Hedge Witches (practitioners of herbal Witchcraft) alike. Land blessings called upon faerie and elf, and saints and trees. The reality is there was no great divide for nearly 600 years. And for hundreds of years a syncretized form of religion flourished – a very eclectic version, which entwined ancient indigenous ways with the teachings of the New Christ and formed a relatively peaceful path, layering aspects of the New Ways over a solid and magical foundation of the Old Ways. Herbal remedies, midwifery, folkloric beliefs and oral history combined to form a concoction of faith that was, at times, not so far removed from the beliefs of the past.

The Church, in fact, had proclaimed that Witchcraft was a myth (despite the Bible devoting a chapter to the Witch of Endor) and that those who believed in such beings were merely falling into the belief systems of the pagan 'past' – even while working within the very festivals and days, the traditions and the Magick it said were myth. But the Church was busy – very busy – from around 600AD dealing with its own internal issues. Catholicism had its own rifts and chasms: Was the seat of the Church Rome, or was it more universal? Was the first saint Peter, or was Paul to be more revered? Ought the Druidal hybrid that was the Celtic Church, the same Church that kept Goddess Brigid and made her a Saint, make worshipping her more acceptable – or was it too pagan? Heresy was the great crime to fight, and as the Dark Ages gave way to the medieval era, the focus shifted to those who dwelled outside of the borders of Christian lands. This is despite the Old Testament, which specifically warned people off consulting with those who could cast spells, raise spirits – all the talents of the Biblical Witch of Endor who you are about to discover.

The Bible's Beautiful, Compassionate Witch of Endor

In the Old Testament is a bizarre story of King Saul consulting with a woman who has come to be known as The Witch of Endor. King Saul, a King of Israel, was said to be profoundly against 'unnatural' crafts like those of the Witch, Wise Woman and necromancer – or, as they are known today, mediums. He had spent his reign effectively driving out anyone who worked with spirits, or herbs, or Wise Women in general. Until he needed one, of course. Saul had relied upon the prophet Samuel for guidance, and when Samuel passed, Saul became lost, falling into despair. Desperate to have the guidance of his old friend back, he turned to a Witch, a woman who lived high in the mountains, deep within a cave, far away from demanding humans. This one last Witch is visited by Saul, who travels the vast distance to her in disguise, and she raises the spirit of Samuel from the dead so the King can ask Samuel his questions. Samuel's spirit is distressed by being disturbed from his rest, and chastises Saul for further angering God by having the Witch raise him up. Saul absolutely believes this is Samuel, by the way – he recognises the voice, and he knows his old friend is not happy with him at all. Samuel goes on to

predict that Saul will perish when he goes into battle the next day, as will his troops and his son, all of whom will be with Samuel soon enough in the land of the dead.

Saul is not pleased with this at all, and breaks down crying. But he knows that his friend's spirit speaks the truth, as he is repeating an earlier prophecy. The Witch comforts the grief-stricken Saul, feeds him (he is famished and worn out from the two-day journey to reach her) and she lays him down in her own bed so he can restore himself for the long journey home.

Saul, as prophesied, goes to war against the Philistines, for all that has set this war in motion took place long ago, when he ignored Samuel's first warnings. His army is slaughtered, his son falls, and Saul is terribly wounded. Knowing he disobeyed God, ignored the wisdom of Samuel, and sought advice from the Witch, he commits suicide by falling on his sword, unable to bear going on amidst the ruins of his life.

It's a curious story. The Witch – or the necromancer or medium – is portrayed so beautifully. She is adept, she is compassionate, and she is truthful. For this passage to have survived in the Bible tells us something of the ambiguous relationships between Magickal women and the Patriarchs of the Old Testament and the Hebrews. To this day, this chapter of the Book of Samuel is argued over by Christians, again and again. And yet there she is, the Witch of Endor – kind, able, and honest. A Wise Woman for the ages. Fans of the delicious 1960s television classic *Bewitched* may also be tickled to know that Samantha Stevens' mother was named after the Witch of the Old Testament – Endora.

Because of the influence of this biblical story, the
enduring appeal of folk magic and the Old Ways, and the
syncretic forms of Magick still in popular use, prosecuting
people for Witchcraft was relatively uncommon, until the
early fourteenth century when a series of natural disasters
left half the population dead and the other half barely
holding on.

Famine, War and Pestilence

There was a mini ice age on the planet in the early 1300s –
great glaciers crept across Northern Europe, temperatures
dropped, infant deaths soared, old and weary ones were
picked off by starvation and disease, women died in
childbirth and all succumbed to fever and hunger. In the
midst of the climate change came crop failures and animal
deaths, which in turn created famine, which in turn was
followed by war – the Hundred Years' War consumed
France and life became hard and frightening, and short and
painful for most people throughout Western Europe and
the British Isles.

Then came an apocalypse. The plague – a swift, lethal
disease landed in the west, and life would never be the
same again. Known as the Black Death because of the
disfiguring black boils that erupted on its victims, this
disease arrived from the east via trader's ships in Sicily
in 1346. Highly contagious, an utterly unprepared and

undernourished populace was easy pickings for the plague.
Carried by rats, upon which fleas feasted, which then bit
humans, the Black Death ruthlessly carved its way through
Italy, then France, spread then to the northern lands, leapt
the sea to Britain and Ireland, turned south to annihilate
the populations of Spain and Portugal. Within five years,
25 million people were dead. Entire towns perished.
Combine this calamity with the Crusades, and the famine,
and the crop failures, and the fierce winters and wars that
had drained money from the coffers of local landholders,

and it is little wonder that people began to hunt for a reason – something, anything – to make sense of this run of misfortune. This rapid succession of dreadful events forever changed the restless alliance between those who practised the Old Ways, and Christians. The Church proclaimed that God had abandoned his people because they had not completely eradicated the old religion. The Devil, they said, was loose in the land, set free by the sympathy still given to those not yet claimed by Christ. The Devil was behind the curses of pestilence and famine, fever and death. Magick, they said, was the Devil's method, and Witches and Wizards were his instruments.

~~~

Practical Magick

Why not work with your own version of the land charm, and make a Magickal poultice and bless your working tools?

Take, at sundown,
One part full-cream milk
One part honey

One part fennel
One part cinnamon
Three drops of frankincense

Chant the following over this concoction nine times:

Earth Mother, Mother of all
Who all the world does adore
Let me prosper, thrive and grow
Bless my work, let it flow
Bring to me the truest riches
I'll honour you with words and wishes
I thank you now for all that shall come
I'll bless my work, with you, with Sun

At sunrise, anoint your chosen tools, area and 'plough the field' with the Great Mother's blessing!

You may wish to anoint your computer, your phone, a special pen or a desk if you work with those tools. Or, you could anoint your kitchen, or an area of your home that represents your own personal source of abundance.

You may also wish to sprinkle some of this blessed concoction in a garden, or at your front door.

The fennel seeds are a lovely touch to use, as working with fennel seeds, according to the Nine Herbs Charm, is one of the most powerful ways to ward off negative energy.

Merlin – The Wild Wizard of Wales

From Green Man to Kingmaker

The Dark Ages – 1400

~᷽~

THERE IS, in a wild, cold land, a great cliff with a stark, fierce face carved into its profile by the wind and the rain and the endless waves of centuries. This stern face gazes out

towards the Atlantic from its home in north Cornwall, staring into the west, the land of legend. Beneath its forbidding watch lies a cave through which thousands of pilgrims in search of a myth have ventured. In the inky darkness is an unmistakable atmosphere, one of Magick and mystery, which has earned the cave its reputation as the enchanted dwelling of the legendary Merlin, the great Magician.

Merlin's cave lies beneath Tintagel Castle, a romantic ruin spread over a dramatic peninsula. Tintagel is said to be King Arthur's birthplace, and the site where the most famous of Wizards wove together strands of magic to save Britain from the Saxon invaders in the fourth century.

ᔐᔑ

There are so many legends surrounding this being known as Merlin. Did he really exist? Is he simply a dream – a vision which we long to bring to life, an archetype we summon in the hope that there have been such fantastic and enigmatic persons in our history? Or is this man we call 'Merlin' a myth, a kind of literary fantasy? Is he an amalgam of real-life ancient mystics and learned druids, of chieftain's advisors, of the wandering wise men known as Druids?

When we begin to dig a little deeper, we see that Merlin, the man, is as elusive as the mist and dragons he was said to rule in the legends. In some versions of the tales he is a man

born of both faery and human. It is believed he lives beneath
the castle of Tintagel to this day. Others claim he rests
beneath Glastonbury Tor alongside Arthur; the French say
he remains trapped in the gnarled roots of a great enchanted

tree in the forest of Broceliande in Brittany, and the Welsh claim he rests with the red and the white dragons beneath the Snowdonia Mountains (also known as Eryri). To ask if Merlin is 'real' and, if so, where he was born and where did he die amounts to asking which of the tales of King Arthur is 'real', and that long and arduous quest is better suited for another book.

Perhaps all we can say for sure is that there is a legend that has its roots in a distant and almost unknowable reality, and we have kept what is most important to us – the archetype of the equally wise and Magickal sage who advises the chosen King, and is loyal to the land, to the tribe and to the ways he calls his own.

A Great Shift Takes Place

In the years between 380AD and 408AD the Romans abandoned Britain, overwhelmed by the increasing incursion of the Saxons from the north, and battling invasions by the Visigoths at home. The Romans left after nearly 350 years of treating Britain as a client-kingdom, systematically destroying tribes, languages, traditions, chieftains and the druids. They left behind them a fractured and wounded Britain, struggling to regain its identity and lacking in leadership, its Old Ways – the indigenous practices of faith, farming, culture, law, family and tribe – threatened by the introduction of Roman gods, armies, taxes, wine and social status, which dishonoured the women of Britain who had previously been warriors and fiercely respected. Christianity had recently been introduced, and had further eroded the Druids – the learned, wise ones (both men and women) who were the Lawkeepers, the diplomats, the ambassadors and the organisers of battle.

Within the epoch known as the Dark Ages, Britain's tribal structures had been fractured by the invasions from Rome, with Christianity beginning to take hold and melding with the ancient Celtic path. The men of the north had also integrated with settlements of farmers, but this uneasy culture disintegrated into tribe against tribe, and pressure from renewed invasions from the Vikings and the Saxons.

Then Saxon hordes poured in from the continent, from lands we would now call northern Germany. Some 200,000 warriors arrived, seeking and claiming good farming land, slaughtering inhabitants, and bringing a different spiritual path to the already fractured Old Ways of Britain.

Merlin – Shapeshifting

In some of the tales, Merlin is a shapeshifter, able to rule the elements and change into various animals, including falcons and hawks. Merlin is also the name of a small falcon, dark-feathered and barrel-tailed, found within Britain and worked with in traditional falconry. Merlins were prized for their fierce intelligence, ability to interact with humans, and sublime hunting skills. The Druids had many animals which they regarded as sacred, and far-sighted birds of prey were greatly esteemed. When a Merlin appears to you as a totem, it is a message to your soul to see things from an enlightened perspective – falcons are creatures of the sun, day predators, and they can see even with all the brightness about them. They also remind us to look at our lives and any issues from a higher perspective. Merlin, the Wizard, is similarly able to see the big picture in all circumstances, and can help us to truly observe what is taking place within a situation.

Merlin was also the name given to the head of the Druids, for a time – so there were perhaps many Merlins, many of these beings who led the wise ones, and who guided ordinary folk in the great matters of Britain, northern and western France, northern Spain and all throughout the lands that have come to be known as Celtic.

A strong leader to unite the fragmented tribes and the people and drive back the invaders was desperately needed. One true King to unite the Britons under one sword must come to save the island of Albion. And according to legend this King was *created* for those dark times – and this creation was masterminded by the Wizard, the Druid, the magician, Merlin.

Merlin Officially Enters History

In his 1136 work *The History of the Kings of Britain* (Historia Regum Britanniae), a young Welsh church cleric named Geoffrey of Monmouth claimed to have received an ancient manuscript in 'the tongue of the Britons'. He claimed to have translated this and added some of his own research, which created a direct line between King Arthur and the current King of the time, Henry I. This discovery was embraced and Geoffrey was rewarded by being made a Bishop of the Church, and his *History of the Kings of Britain*, which draws heavily on the Mabinogion, druidry and oral legends of the west countries, was accepted as truth until the 1700s, after which his methods were called into question.

Who Were the Druids?

It is almost certain that the being we now call Merlin was a Druid, perhaps their leader for a time. Perhaps he was the first leader of this name, and from that time forth, the leader of that ancient caste of priests, healers, seers and lawmakers, male and female, was known as the Merlin.

What did Druids do?

The wise Druids read the stars, the trees, the animals, the stones, and protected these natural things. They saw them as they truly are: sacred. Today's Druids, including historian Ronald Hutton, believes that Druids were divided into three kinds of groups – bards, ovates and Druids. The modern British Druid organisation, OBOD (Organisation of Bards, Ovates and Druids) has over 35,000 members worldwide, growing yearly. In October 2010, Druidry was recognised as an official religion in the United Kingdom.

The British Druidic tradition is very real, and ancient. In a world without the kind of communication we have today, people relied on these men and women to travel from tribe to tribe, conducting ceremonies, telling stories – essentially spreading the news. They held the history and geneology of the land. They were Shamans, who had a foot in both this world and the otherworld, and they helped connect people back to nature, to the wheel of time, and to what is truly important.

What do Druids believe?

To the Druids, everything on this planet – everything – is a repository of consciousness, and we too have the facility to be so connected with the natural world and with our own innate psychic abilities as expressed through the natural world and through our senses.

Whatever his sources, this Welshman's work achieved many things. It was an immense and successful work of propoganda – it lent King Henry I an air of romance, a sense of credibility by association, and gave him an important connection with King Arthur, which was a priceless lineage to hold. It also introduced the legend of Myrddin (Welsh, pronounced *Mierth-en*) which over time became Merlin. Geoffrey of Monmouth also published *Vita Merlini*, or *The Life of Merlin*, and *The Prophecies of Merlin* – a kind of collection of predictions he said he had gleaned from the ancient manuscripts.

So, we have the first widely known written work featuring a fully fleshed Merlin. Geoffrey, a deeply religious man of the Church, seemed incapable of imagining that Merlin was of the Old Ways, or born of faery and human, and stated within his pages that the Wizard was the son of the coupling of a devil and a Christian woman. He drew

MERLIN AND VIVIEN

upon the great tales of Wales, which included the legends of
Myrddin Wyllt – or Merlin the Wild – a wise man of the
forest, a shamanic Druid who spoke the languages of the
plants and the trees and could read the movements of the
animals and the birds; who shunned human interaction and
lived in accordance with the wills of the Old Gods. Geoffrey
conjured Merlin the Wild in his Histories, and claimed he
had found new documents telling of the part Merlin had
played in the Arthurian history.

Thus it is due to Geoffrey of Monmouth that we
experience the first ever record of Merlin's ingenuity. The
tale has evolved over the years, until what we have now
is a version of Merlin in which we see he is able to think
quickly, see through illusions, explain the meaning of omens
to Kings, and change the course of history. In the first tale
in the Histories, Geoffrey recounts a King Vortigern of
Wales, who is attempting to build a castle upon a ridge
of the Snowdonia Mountains, in Gwynedd. This was the
most far-flung part of his kingdom, and his purpose was
to build a great fort that would protect him and his tribe
from the Saxons. But every time the castle walls went up,
a great earthquake would shake the mountains – and the
castle walls would crumble. Builders were maimed and killed
beneath the falling stones and Vortigern, dispirited, turned
to his wise men, who declared a great sacerifice must be
made to the mountain. The sacrifice must be a young man,

born of no human father, but of a human mother, and he
must bleed upon the earth, so the mountain's appetite for
destruction would be quelled while it drank the blood of the
young man of no human father.

Vortigern's men searched, and finally brought to their
chieftain a wild youth of the forest, with hair twisted like
branches and beard brimming with oak leaves. His wild
eyes stared into the King's, his tall body strong and proud
though he was in chains. That sacrifice was none other than
Myrddin Emrys, or Merlin, and he knew the secrets of the
land. He spoke to Vortigern the words he had needed to
hear for so long. Merlin had seen in a vision a great pool
of water beneath the mountains, and within that pool two
dragons did battle: one red, and one white. And while they
battled, there could never be peace within that realm, and
Vortigern's – or any King's – castle could never be built, and
his tribe would never be safe from the fierce invaders.

King Vortigern challenged the wise men to reveal the
meaning of this vision. But they could not.

And the young man, born of no human father, said that
the pool beneath the mountains was the symbol of the
great land of the Britons, and the two dragons were two
kingdoms. The red dragon represented the tribes of the west,
led by King Vortigern, and the white dragon represented
the tribes of the Saxons, who already occupied the east of
Britain. And he explained to the King that this mountain

MORGAN LE FAY CASTS AWAY THE SCABBARD

was no place to build his castle – that another King would come, and the Saxons would be driven forever from the land they had invaded.

And Vortigern felt the truth of the Wild Man's words, and did not take his life, and made him his Merlin – for the young man was called Myrddin Emrys, and the mountain in time was called after his own name.

The Pendragon Lines

There are two great energy lines that run through Britain, which have been dowsed and mapped since the 1920s. On these lines lie many ancient, sacred sites – some Arthurian – and the energies themselves are said to be both red and white, and masculine and feminine.

Along those two lines of energy – the red and the white Pendragon lines – lies Glastonbury Tor. Beneath Glastonbury Tor lie a red and a white spring, two completely interwoven yet independent sources of fresh water that have very different mineral properties. Could these two mystical springs be the red and white dragons of Merlin's prophecies? Because Glastonbury Tor has experienced earthquakes, some have even said that it is here that Vortigern attempted to build his mighty defence against the Saxons and not in Wales. The Arthurian connection with Glastonbury is very strong, with many saying the Tor was the Isle of Avalon before the inland sea receded, and within Glastonbury Abbey a grave was found in the 1200s – at the height of Henry's II's desire to connect his reign with that of Arthur's. The grave contained both a woman's body and a man's body, and an inscription upon a mounted sword above the grave was said to translate to: 'Here lies the body of King Arthur and his Queen Gwynevere.'

Many renowned mystics and occultists, included Dion Fortune and many members of the Golden Dawn, believe the Holy Grail and King Arthur himself lie sleeping beneath the mighty Glastonbury Tor.

Merlin and the Origins of Arthur

One of the most famous tales in Geoffrey's *History of the Kings of Britain* is about Merlin's creation of Arthur, the future King of the Britons. Merlin is said to have consulted with the Druids and the Wise Men and Women of the Old Ways, and it was agreed among them that a future king must spring from the right people – those who have the blood of the Old Ways running through their veins. Merlin arranges a meeting between Igraine, the wife of Gorloise of Cornwall, and Uther Pendragon, a chieftain of the east.

Igraine is a good woman, who has a child already with
Gorloise of Cornwall (more likely to have been the chieftain
of the region, and perhaps the chieftain who built the oldest
remnants of the Tintagel Castle). That daughter is Morgan,
who would become the legendary Morgan le Fay (see the
breakout box on page 36).

Igraine and Uther Pendragon are drawn to each other, bound by Magick and an even deeper connection – that of enduring, lifetimes-long love. After the death of Ambrosius, who preceded Arthur's father and whom Merlin had become adviser to, the chieftains gather and choose Uther to be the next leader of the Britons. Gorloise, furious at not receiving the title, and seeing the new King's attraction for his wife, returns to Cornwall.

He is called to fight alongside his new King, and Igraine, while at home, sees a vision of her husband betraying Uther, and sends him a warning in a vision. They fight, and in a great battle, Uther kills Gorloise.

Uther then goes to Cornwall to claim Igraine as his bride. In order to pass by Gorloise's soldiers, who have forbidden Igraine to leave Tintagel Castle, Merlin conjures a great mist, which helps Uther to shapeshift, changing his face to the face of Gorloise, and he passes the guards, rides across the bridge to the castle and enters it – proclaimed as the returning Duke.

A little more than nine months later a son is born on the winter solstice at Tintagel, and he is named Arthur, for the bear in the sky at his time of birth and for the courage he will need. He is the son of love, the son of old blood, and the son of Magick, and Merlin will watch over him and take him under his cloak, and train him in the ways of the wild old ones, in order to ready him for a world that is falling to pieces once again.

Meet Arthur's Sister, Morgan le Fay

Arthur's older half-sister has been painted as evil by nearly all Arthurian scholars, including Thomas Malory, who re-ignited interest in the Arthurian legends through his book, *Le Morte d'Arthur*. But other parts of her story indicate that Morgan was a wise woman, a Lady of the Lake, and a priestess of the Triple Goddess. In various versions of the tale she unwittingly conceives of a child during the Great Rite at Beltane. When she and her brother re-enact the Great Rite, the sexual Magick returns to the land its fecundity. Their coupling is nearly always seen as diabolical – and often, Merlin is held accountable for bringing them together. Christian tellers of the legend have tended to recreate the character of Morgan as an evil Witch-temptress, rather than the Priestess Witch she was, and in Geoffrey of Monmouth's Histories she is described as a necromancer and a shapeshifter, able to transform into a raven at will. She ultimately took her brother Arthur from the battlefield of Cammlyn, where he was fatally wounded by their own son, and returned the dying King to Avalon, or Glastonbury Tor – where he sleeps to this day, awaiting his lands great need – or perhaps still undergoing great healing.

Merlin Takes Root in Popular Consciousness

Merlin as a figure in literature began to appear more regularly in the 1200s – in prose poems, and then in the ever-growing body of work that became the Arthurian canon. From Chretien de Troyes' tales of Camelot through to Tennyson's Idylls of the King, the way that Merlin was portrayed was in the hands of the writer, the one who was, in so many ways, summoning the spirit of the Wizard of Britain.

But his truth and his deep roots are in the ways of Druidry, in the schools of the bard, the ovate and the Druid. His truth is that in the west of Britain, where the Romans did not decimate the Old Ways, and where the Saxons only penetrated a little, there is a repository of wisdom in the language, the legends and the treasure of those places that holds the indigenous knowledge of the ancient people of these isles.

Perhaps the tale of Merlin's cave, filled with treasure, is a metaphor – a tale telling us that the fortunes of Britain are in the blood of the people, in its origins and old languages, in its folk tales and traditions; that the riches are in the west, the places that remained untouched and truly themselves. And Merlin, that great Wizard, lets the bell of the cave ring for us all, and rolls out the wisdom when we connect deeply with the Old Ways, and with our own blood.

The Treasure of Merlin

In Geoffrey of Monmouth's tales of Merlin, he retells a strange legend about the great Wizard. When leaving Wales to create and bring to the throne the rightful King of the Britons, one who could unite the tribes and fight the Saxons and keep the Old Ways, Myrddin was said to place his great treasures – a chalice and wand, staffs and scrying tools, coin and gemstones – into a great golden cauldron, and hide it deep within a cave in the most remote of mountain ranges. He rolled a huge stone – or levitated it – into place before the cave, and with his Magick caused the grass and flowers and trees to grow over the entrance in intricate knots, which formed a part of a secret language only he could understand.

It is said that the treasure lies there to this day, and that when the rightful heir to this treasure comes to Dinas, bells will ring out and the cave will open itself up and offer the treasures to the one who can wield them for the good of all.

To this day, these treasures have never been found.

Magickal Practicum

Merlin is said to be able to come to those who seek his assistance, particularly those with an understanding of the natural world, and the ability to connect with their own psychic powers. If you would like your own intuition to be keener, sharper; your sixth-sensory capacity alert and ready to help you, call on Merlin! He can also help you to tune in to and adjust your psychic gifts: to turn your power up or down. If you feel bombarded with messages, respectfully ask him to make them simpler, clearer, and to come at particular times. (Be ready for communications with the plant and animal realms after connecting with Merlin.)

Invocation to Merlin

Say three times: *Honoured Merlin, great sage and Wizard of the Old Ways, dissolve all blocks which allow me to see, hear, smell, taste and otherwise, in all ways experience my psychic powers. Allow me to see the signs which are all around me, and to read them with clarity, courage, detachment, compassion and for the highest good of all concerned. Allow me to know that it is now safe to be fully functioning clairvoyantly, clairsentiently, clairaudiently and through my dreams and every aspect of the natural world and the etheric planes. Allow me to trust the messages when they come, and pass them on without becoming involved in the message itself, and to know that this process is sacred, safe and for the highest good of all concerned.*

Bring the Hammer Down

How the Burning Times Began

1400—1500

❧

'All Witchcraft comes from carnal lust, which is in women insatiable.'

The Malleus Maleficarum, The Hammer of the Witches, 1484

ONCE UPON a time, in a pretty town called Werzberg, Germany, there lived a beautiful young woman. Her hair was long and gold as flax, her eyes were blue as a clear summer sky, her face and form uncommon in their loveliness. Her smile was broad and bright and freely given, and at nineteen years of age, she had never been touched by disease or anything other than ordinary misfortune, and thus she was regarded as somewhat unnaturally lucky by the townspeople. She worked hard at the brewers, and it was her job to bring and place the herbs into the beer's brew, and to keep the cauldron from burning too bright or too low.

One day, she gathered the herbs for the beer, but no-one was in the fields as they usually were. As she walked through the streets she noticed groups of people gathered, clustered together, and the wary glances cast her way. She took the herbs to the brewers, but no-one was about their work as they would usually be. When she saw a friend that evening, she was told that a great man had come to Werzberg, and he had found that the Devil himself was loose in their streets. Her friend whispered that people were going to burn and she rubbed her eyes so red with sleepless nights from worry about it. The brewer's girl tried hard not to think about this. It made her uneasy in her bed that night and distracted her in her work the following day. And that was how mistakes could be made. But her mind kept drifting to the horrible events her friend had said were about to take place. And even though she pushed the thoughts away, within a week the burnings began. A little girl was accused and tried, and then burned as a witch. Nine years old. Then another little girl, even younger. A little boy, even younger again. Three minstrels were next. A whole group of travelling players. The butcher, his wife and their son. Four innkeepers. Fourteen vicars. Two choristers of the cathedral. The apothecary, his wife and his daughter.

Something was wrong within the town, she knew, but she kept her lips tightly shut and went about her business, and tried not to meet the eyes of the Witchfinders, who had moved into the town upon the order of the powerful man who was now watching for the Devil in the town.

The young woman slept fitfully, hearing the children's screams echo through her dreams.

One day she was awoken by a knock at her door, and was told that the beer she had made was spoiled, and foul, and dangerous. That this meant she had intended to kill others, on behalf of her master, Satan. Half asleep, with her nightshirt on, she was taken. She was tortured. Weeks later she was taken to the square in front of the church devoted to Our Lady, and it would be her turn to burn.

I've created a story around this young woman, because we don't know a great deal about her. But she was real, and her name was Gobel Babelin – recorded on the court transcripts as 'the prettiest girl in town'. Others did not have their names recorded. Their descriptions are bare, and bizarre. 'A little maiden of nine', 'A pretty young woman of 24', 'A girl of fifteen'.

Perhaps their names were not considered important enough to record. But we know their ages, and that they died most cruelly and unjustly.

It is impossible to read of Europe's trials for Witchcraft without being repelled by the torture, violence and the mass

executions. In Gobel's little town of Wurzburg, the sky turned black with smoke for nearly two years. The cloud did not disperse, and the choking of the remaining inhabitants was said to be the result of the injustice done to the thousand-strong people burned alive in the public square. On one day alone, 192 were sent to the stake. Wurzburg may have been a hotbed, but right across Germany, France, Denmark and Finland, the night skies were alight with the flaming bodies of innocent men, women and children.

The Origins of Terror

How did this come to be? Why were thousands of women and children and men seized and murdered within so short a time?

From 1073–1085 Pope Gregory VII had ruled the Church with a level of reason and decency that led to Europe being relatively tolerant for nearly two hundred years after his passing. He proclaimed he did not believe in the existence of Witches, nor in the ability of devils to inhabit a person. So what had changed?

For it was not a normal state of affairs, the Witch craze, the 'hysterique' as the French called it, that took hold of all of Europe in the 1500s, reaching epic heights in the 1600s when James I declared that practising Witchcraft was punishable by death (see pages 102–105).

Were Men Ever Witches?

Within Hungary, Denmark, Britain, and later North America, the majority of people accused, tried and executed for Witchcraft were women. But in some nations, most of the victims were men. In Iceland, nearly all the accused were men, over half in Estonia, and at least half of the accused were men in Finland. There are some extreme cases in peripheral regions of Europe, with men accounting for ninety per cent of the accused. It is undoubtedly true, however, that every single one of the court officials, judges and executioners was a man.

'Ah, the woe and the misery of it.'

The series of natural disasters and terrible pestilences that swept across Europe in the fourteenth century created an environment of fear, paranoia and suspicion. Fear is a hungry demon, and it has its needs, and it must find someone or something to blame for the deaths, the sick animals, the failing crops, the longer, colder Winters. The Church pointed the finger at the remnants of the Old Ways, and so the practices of the cunning-men, the brews of the herbalists and the midwives, the chants of the charm makers and the

potion brewers, the tools of fortune tellers and the singers and
dancers and storytellers who loved the trees and the stones
and the land more than God were found to be the bringers of
doom. The Church had found its mark, and fear of the Devil
took root in the hearts of otherwise good men and women.

By autumn of 1629, the Chancellor of the Prince-Bishop
of Wurzburg wrote to a friend:

'As to the affair of the witches ... no words can do justice
to it. Ah, the woe and the misery of it. There are law
students to be arrested. The Prince-Bishop has over forty
students who are soon to be pastors; among them thirteen
or fourteen are said to be witches. A few days ago a Dean
was arrested; two others who were summoned have fled.
The notary of our Church consistory, a very learned man,
was yesterday arrested and put to the torture. The richest,
most attractive, most prominent, of the clergy are already
executed. A week ago a maiden of nineteen was executed,
of whom it is everywhere said that she was the fairest in
the whole city, and was held by everybody a girl of singular
modesty and purity. She will be followed by seven or
eight others of the best and most attractive persons ... To
conclude this wretched matter, there are children of three
and four years, to the number of three hundred, who are
said to have had intercourse with the Devil. I have seen
put to death children of seven, promising students of ten,
twelve, fourteen, and fifteen. I cannot and must not write
more of this misery.'

To Be Put to the Question

How did any of this become possible? There is one document
written by one religious scribe who, perhaps more than any
other, gave credence to the claims that cost so many lives. In
1487 an enthusiastic inquisitor of the Dominican Order of
monks, Heinrich Kramer, completed a legal document that
changed the way Witches and Wizards were viewed right
across Christendom. Highly influential, it paved the way
for torture, mass executions, and the persecution of anyone
perceived to be following the old religion.

The *Malleus Maleficarum* – Latin for 'The Hammer of
the Witches' – made it the law to believe and to agree that
Witches were the Devil's creatures, who must be sought
out, and destroyed. The acceptance of this document across
Europe changed the law so that any practice of the Old
Ways became heresy, punishable by death. In fact, the
disbelief in Witches or their evil was declared a heresy, and
thus those who objected to these new laws were also swiftly
silenced, either by death or through fear.

A work in three acts, part one lays out, in hysterical
language, the abomination that the Church considered
Witches and anyone who renounced Catholicism, but most
especially Witches, to be working with the Devil. They even
suggested these people enjoyed sexual intercourse with the
Devil. Part two is an imagined catalogue of Witches' habits,
familiars and practices, and part three lays out ways to

MALLEVS
MALEFICARVM,
MALEFICAS ET EARVM
haeresim frameâ conterens,

EX VARIIS AVCTORIBVS COMPILATVS,
& in quatuor Tomos iustè distributus.

*QVORVM DVO PRIORES VANAS DÆMONVM
versutias, præstigiosas eorum delusiones, superstitiosas Strigimagarum
cæremonias, horrendos etiam cum illis congressus; exactam denique
tam pestiferæ sectæ disquisitionem, & punitionem complectuntur.
Tertius praxim Exorcistarum ad Dæmonum, & Strigimagarum male-
ficia de Christi fidelibus pellenda; Quartus verò Artem Doctrinalem,
Benedictionalem, & Exorcismalem continent.*

TOMVS PRIMVS.
Indices Auctorum, capitum, rerúmque non desunt.

Editio nouissima, infinitis penè mendis expurgata; cuique accessit Fuga
Dæmonum & Complementum artis exorcisticæ.

*Vir siue mulier, in quibus Pythonicus, vel diuinationis fuerit spiritus, morte moriatur
Leuitici cap. 10.*

LVGDVNI,
Sumptibus CLAVDII BOVRGEAT, sub signo Mercurij Galli.

M. DC. LXIX.
CVM PRIVILEGIO REGIS.

discover, prosecute, strip, shave, examine, prick, torture, convict, then execute – through burning – Witches. It declares that any person who asks help of a Witch – a charm or a potion to help grow crops, keep their animals alive, come safely through illness – was working with the Devil, and was sinning. This, it  proclaimed, was why God had sent the cold, the famine, the plague. The only solution was to find Witches and destroy them – and their accomplices. One fascinating aspect of the document is that it, for the first time, feminised the word relating to Witch – *maleficarum* – thus establishing that Witches were women in the main.

And so the slaughter of Eve's daughters began.

There are so many cases to examine, too many to mention. We often imagine that these terrible events are in the past, and imagine even more foolishly that the Witch burnings are over. But they are not. Within countries throughout Africa that are swiftly becoming radically Christianised, the burning of presumed Witches takes place with a horrible regularity. And in case Western nations believe that they are so far removed from such things, know that as recently as March 1995 an Anglican vicar in Lincolnshire, England, publicly called for female priests to be burnt at the stake as Witches. The word 'Witch' is still used as a term of insult and disgust. This is how deep the fear runs, how strongly it remains.

The Dreaded Matthew Hopkins – The Witch Hunter General

Matthew Hopkins is infamous as the most disciplined, organised and remorseless Witch Hunter of Britain, a man whose incredible court-and-Church given powers led to more people being executed for Witchcraft within his three-year reign of terror than had been executed for the same 'crime' in the preceding 100 years. Almost certainly a sadist, Hopkins' heyday was between 1644 and 1647. His appointment was due in great part to the success of his widely-distributed pamphlet, *The Discovery of Witches*,

a publication featuring his own bizarre imaginings, which
Hopkins claimed were the practices of Witches and
their familiars.

The Witch's Cat and Other Familiars

During the 300 years known now as the Burning Times, it was not only women and men – and children – who were burned. Witches' familiars were also tried and executed, thousands upon thousands of times. A Witch's familiar was considered to be an animal that worked alongside the Witch, a kind of conduit for the Devil. Of course this is paranoia of the greatest kind. Magickal alliances between animals and humans are hardly rare. But in the Burning Times, the keeping of a cat, or a bird, a snake or a hare, was enough to inflame suspicion. Once accusations were made, lives were ruined, if not taken altogether.

But within the sinister pages of the *Malleus Maleficarum* lies a story where it was claimed a Witch took the shape of a black cat to harass a servant. This led to the belief that a black cat was almost certainly a Witch in disguise. Cats came to be so identified with Witches and Witchcraft that throughout Europe in the 1600s there were mass burnings of live cats. St John the Baptist's feast day was one such day when cats would meet this awful fate in mass 'executions'. The most cruel were the bonfires of Paris, where thousands of cats were incinerated alive.

In Britain, cats (and occasionally dogs, or birds) were regularly tried for Witchcraft, and if found guilty – which they almost inevitably were – execution was carried out by the court.

One of the Witchfinder General's most infamous trials was that of poor Elizabeth Clark. During the trial, Hopkins offered as evidence her five familiars – animals who lived with Elizabeth, animals who, Hopkins claimed, drew power from the Devil in order to offer this energy up to their evil mistress. (A familiar, in Magickal terms, is an animal who works in partnership with a person to lend them their instinctive wisdom – thus a dog could lend its powerful ability to track, a cat its dignity, a horse its speed, a bird its perspective, the stag its nobility, for example. Some of this is considered to be literal – and some of this is considered to be a part of trance work, and somewhat metaphorical.)

Therefore, accused in the court was a squirrel, a spaniel who had lost his legs, three kittens called Holt, Sack and Sugar, a black rabbit, and a full-grown cat called Pyewacket. Hopkins' evidence during Elizabeth's trial was that no human could possibly care for so many animals – and no human could have given Pyewacket its name. It's hard

to read the descriptions of the trial without wondering
if Elizabeth Clark was simply a wise woman who loved
animals, preferring their company to that of malevolent
humans. Thousands of women, some men, and even children
died thanks to Hopkins's zealous pursuit of imagined evil.
Perhaps, in the end, some justice was done, for Hopkins
himself was arrested by angry townsfolk as he headed
towards their quiet homes one day. He was tried as a Witch,
and found guilty – for only a Witch, the folk said, would
know of so many others.

A more fitting end is hard to imagine.

How Many People Died?

This is a very difficult question to answer with any real
accuracy. The highest counts, which were made in the 1970s,
were that some nine million people were executed during
what is now known broadly as the Burning Times. Those
numbers have recently been revised as the scholarship in
this area has increased dramatically – consequently the
numbers now vary between academics. Some claim 100,000,
some closer to 300,000, but these numbers tend to discount
people who died in prison, those who committed suicide
prior to execution, those who were in smaller villages where
record keeping was poor, and those whose deaths were
deliberately attributed to another cause because the victim

did not receive a trial, which was law. Most official numbers are based on accused witches who survived imprisonment, trial and torture, and lived long enough to be executed.

Practickal Magick –
Take Refuge Beneath the Witch's Tree

Before the Burning Times set the Western world alight, it was said that if a Witch was persecuted or hunted, she could find refuge beneath the branches of the Rowan tree. The Rowan would render her invisible, and even help her to remain 'unseen' by anyone wishing her ill-luck. The Rowan is a Magickal tree according to the lore of the ancient Celts, and oftentimes sprigs of Rowan were kept above Wise Women's doors, or pinned to their cloaks to protect them from those who would do them harm. Strangely, this led to a post Burning Times superstition that Rowan protected people from Witches!

If the working of tree Magick appeals to you, why not grow a protective herb – lemon verbena, rosemary, lavender, or thyme, near your front and back doors. It will lend you some of its powers, and turn away those who approach with malintent.

The Final Fires: Janet Horne

In 1727, Janet Horne, an old woman, described as confused, who had the misfortune to have given birth to a daughter with a malformed hand, was accused with turning that same daughter into a pony to help her escape the Witch Hunters. Janet Horne and her daughter were both imprisoned at the formidable Dornoch jail in Scotland – both were tried and found guilty of Witchcraft. They were sentenced to death – but maybe old Janet somehow worked a wee bit of magick, for her daughter escaped, aided perhaps by sympathetic townspeople who had had enough of seeing the old and the different, the misfits and the rebels, burnt. Perhaps they'd had enough of the Wise Women of their towns perishing in the flames – with their deaths they lost their midwives, their herbalists, and the loss left a huge hole in Britain's villages. But Janet was too old and weakened by prison, torture and trials to run.

The day after her sentencing, the morning after her daughter had fled, old Janet Horne was stripped naked in the streets and rolled in tar. She was placed in a barrel, and it was set alight. And so she died, in a most cruel way. And something about this death disgusted the people. It was wrong. Janet had birthed their babies and healed them when they were sick. She had said the old prayers over the departed. And now she was dead, her daughter was fled, and the inquisitors would move on, and leave them without doctor or Wise Woman.

Something about this death shifted people's minds and hearts. Where did evil lie – in the working of these old people who practised the arts of nature, or in the cruelties and tortures of those who said they did God's work? Whatever the truth, Janet Horne was the last woman burned in Britain. Not the last to be prosecuted under the horrible act – but the last to die in this evil way.

The Wizard of the Burning Times

The Astonishing Tale and Amazing Deeds of Doctor John Dee

1527—1609

❧

A MIDDLE-AGED man with a long dark beard, stiff white ruff and long clever fingers is hurrying to write down words he can barely see on the parchment lit by the guttering candles … He risks a glance at the man opposite him, slumped on a chair, shivering and shaking as strange words fall from his lips. What he speaks of is incomprehensible to most people, and he has no sensibility of speaking a thing at all. Because Edward Kelley is no longer there. The Irish accent is gone, the tone is gone, the sound of his voice has utterly changed … and what remains is a vessel through which pours the voices of the Angels, speaking directly to Doctor John Dee, master mathematician, Elizabethan spy, astrologer, alchemist and magician. His pen dips into the ink again and again and again, attempting to capture every utterance of the messengers from God. He wipes his brow, and watches closely as the connection lapses every now and again, Kelley's head sinking to his chest with exhaustion, body twitching with the effort of this otherworldly communication. But just as it seems their session is over, and Dr Dee is about to awaken the channel from his trance with a little bread and beer, Kelley's body jerks violently, and the Angel's words begin to flow again. Dr Dee's head is searing, aching with fierce concentration, but he pushes on – for what he is writing down are the channelled words of the Angels, who are sharing their Magickal secrets with him through the vessel known as Edward Kelley. Dr John Dee, a servant of God, is enraptured, trembling with the responsibility, straining to hear every glorious word, refusing to stop until the Angels bring this to an end. Finally, after nearly twenty-four hours, Kelley falls silent … the session over at last. Dee calls a servant to take Kelley away and to put him to bed, and to let him sleep for as long as he needs. Alone at last, Dee re-reads the words of the Angels, and the great man begins to weep with the majesty of it all. He makes a note at the end of the entry, overwhelmed, as his heart fills with gratitude.

'Oh my God,' he writes, fighting to calm himself. 'How profounde are these mysteries … I am the pen merely of God, whose Spirit, quickly writing these things through me, I wish and I hope to be …'

Dr John Dee is truly one of the world's most influential and fascinating real-life Wizards. A bona-fide mathematical genius, a political and occult adviser to Elizabeth I, and a dedicated, visionary occultist, Dee bridged the worlds of mystery and politics during a very dangerous age. To this day Dee remains an astonishing character, one who has never lost his hold on the public imagination, and who has never quite garnered the respect he is due. Along with his genius, his passion for the occult and his determination to pierce the veil and connect with the unseen world, Dee created an occult language and system that is more popular today than ever before – Enochian Magick.

During his colourful eighty-two years of life, Dee was arrested at least twice for sorcery and more than twice for treason. Banished from Britain and called home from exile, Dee's obsessions led him through the whole gamut of human experience – the glittering favour of the royal court, great poverty, intense relationships, sex scandals, a beloved family, buried treasure, public condemnation and physical attacks. He was the darling of the powerful and brilliant Elizabeth I and became her watchful eyes and her spy – some say Dee began what was to become, in time, the British Secret Service. He was an outcast, who nevertheless managed to keep his head, follow a scandalous Magickal path and even inspire William Shakespeare to write *The Tempest*, a play featuring a powerful magician, Prospero, modelled on Dee.

That he managed to live as long as he did is testament to his wit, daring and courage – and his lifelong value to Elizabeth I.

❧

Born in Mortlake in 1527, John Dee was a child of rare talents, showing such brilliance in mathematics that he was accepted into Cambridge University at fifteen years of age.

It was at Cambridge that he experienced his first brush with the dangers of his particular brand of genius when he was publicly accused of sorcery. His crime? Dee had created an amazing mechanical flying beetle for a theatrical production – essentially one of the very first robots. It was a taste of what was to be a recurring

theme in this magician's life – a life where he walked the very edges of acceptability, a side effect of being born a Wizard in an age of upheaval, superstition and radical, rapid advances in science.

Despite being shaken by the persecutions at Cambridge, Dee's deeply mystical nature flourished once he moved out into the world. Armed with academia's highest honours, he was led to fellow mystic and scholar Cornelius Agrippa, who began teaching the young Wizard the ways of alchemy and astrology. His unique combination of genius and mysticism led Dee to become convinced of the possibility that a true union with God was possible – a literal ability to speak with God or the Highest Mystic Powers could be achieved, if we simply knew the right way.

His journey to becoming an occult legend began in earnest and his reputation as a brilliant Wizard who could cast accurate horoscopes enabling others to see into their futures began to attract the attention of the rich and very, very powerful.

This was always going to be a dangerous path for Dee, even in the age known as the Enlightenment. Magick and science were still very much the same beast in the 1500s. They were both treated with much caution and you just needed to be on the right side of the Magick. This was an age when investigating science could lead to a charge of Witchcraft – and if found guilty, that crime was punishable by death – but it was slightly before the great height of the Witchcraft era (see previous chapter). A scientist or alchemist or Wizard could practise certain forms of what was considered Magick – if the magician was seen to be working in conjunction with God's will, this was often considered permissible, even if it was not quite respectable. John Dee, doctor of mathematics, master of spies, and genius of Magick, absolutely felt he was doing God's work. Even so, the Merlin of Mortlake walked a very fine line throughout his long and fascinating life.

His sudden fame – and notoriety – truly began when he was officially requested to cast a horoscope for Mary, the Queen of England, a fervent Roman Catholic who burned those who practised Protestantism. Curiously, he was also commissioned to cast for Mary's younger half-sister and potential rival for the throne – Elizabeth. When 'Bloody' Mary discovered that Dee had predicted that her younger sister's destiny was to become Queen, the hapless Wizard was accused of treason – a crime punishable by the most dishonourable and torturous of deaths, drawing and quartering. Dee, with the shadow of execution hanging over him for the second time in his relatively young life, was sent to the Tower. The young Wizard pleaded his case with characteristic verve and brilliance, and was ultimately released by Mary, albeit reluctantly, but remained closely watched and under suspicion for the remainder of Mary's life. This dangerous incident was the greatest stroke of luck Dee could have had – for it endeared him to Elizabeth, who recognized his gift, commitment and loyalty. When she did indeed become the Queen of England in November of 1558, Dee was sent for, and his ascension to the Merlin – the advisor, the Wizard by the side of perhaps the greatest monarch England would ever see, was complete.

With Elizabeth's patronage and protection, Dee was able to pursue his true desires … to immerse himself in the most daring Magickal possibilities of mystical investigations. He wore many faces – an invaluable advisor and diplomat, he advised Elizabeth on the correct date for her coronation to ensure a long and productive reign, and he began to practise

the art of scrying, using crystals, in order to see into the
future for her. But for perhaps the first time, Doctor Dee
was blocked – for this great magician found he was unable
to scry as he would wish, unable to channel the messages
he reached for, but did not effectively receive, and he
became frustrated at his own inability to hear the word of
the Divine. His work as a master of spies and inventor
of instruments of navigation continued, but his ability to
be of assistance to his Queen was frustratingly limited.

And this is where another fabulous character comes into
this tale, one who would both propel Dee's Magickal career
into legend, and irreparably tarnish his reputation.

The Curious Mister Kelley

Dee, in his subtle way, had put the word out that he was
looking for a Magickal companion to work with – someone
who had talents that he lacked. Which was how he met the
alchemist, scryer, medium and channeler, Edward Kelley.
Equal parts rogue, and genuinely talented occultist, Kelley
knew exactly the right way to approach Dee.

In every account, Kelley is described as a charming
Irishman who wore his hair long to hide his ears, which
had been cropped – a common punishment for a thief or
fraudster in the 1500s. Whether Dee knew or cared that the
eloquent and persuasive Kelley's reputation as an alchemist
was exceeded only by his reputation as a man on the

make, we cannot know. What is clear is that their first meeting was such a success that they began to work together almost immediately.

Dee and the Language of the Angels

In Kelley, Dee found his perfect partner – a medium and channeler who would be able to hear or see and receive the pure word of God. Dee's plan was to somehow connect with the pure, undiluted voice of God's messengers – to speak directly with Angels, and to literally reveal and study their language. The Angelic language is often referred to as the Enochian language. The word 'Enochian' is derived from the prophet Enoch, who appears in the Old Testament. Enoch was able to speak directly with the messengers of the Lord – Angels. So the word 'Enochian' really means the pure form of communication with which God spoke to Adam before the temptation, and the fall, and the banishing from the Garden of Eden. Perhaps Dee felt that the reclaiming of this language could return us to a pre-fall state – where we enjoyed the perfect grace of God once again. This was a very fine line to dance – as Dee could be seen to be attempting to counteract humanity's destiny, and to 'save us', which, in the climate of the day, was a domain purely for God. Was Dee setting himself up alongside his own God?

Whatever his reasons, and from all the readings, it seems unlikely he was ego-driven – Dee felt that this Enochian language, this tongue of the Angels, would help humanity by allowing us to connect again with God in a way that would restore our relationship and help free us from the inheritance of Adam's sin. This was radical work, and could be considered prideful at best, sorcery at worst. But it also demonstrates that Dee, while a passionate mystic, was nevertheless a Christian whose desire was to somehow get closer to God, and to free himself from the taint and ignorance of original sin. But using scrying, sorcery, mediumship and necromancy were very suspect methods that could easily have led to questioning and torture, even when you were one of the Virgin Queen's most beloved and valuable subjects.

The Enochian Calls to the Angels

The Angelic language created by – or delivered to – John Dee and Edward Kelley is called Enochian. There are 48 calls – or chanted invocations – in the Enochian language which can be intoned to effectively open the Gates between this world and that of the realm of Angels.

This series of chants can also be regarded as keys – literally the sounds and the combinations pierce the ordinary world and sing directly to the Angels in their own language. They are also accompanied by a series of symbols – which used in combination form messages or sigils – which only the Angels are able to understand.

According to Dee, there were 49 gates of wisdom – but one key was never to be revealed, as one Gate must never be opened.

As well as directly speaking with Angels, the Enochian language and calls could also be worked with to talk to other spirit-beings – even demons. The debate about whether this is good or malevolent Magick has been raging ever since. Whichever it may prove to be in time, it is undoubtedly powerful – and it is worked with for a very good reason. The Enochian practice brings messages unlike any other form of Magick before or since. It is volatile, transformative, complex and almost certainly leads us to contact with beings beyond our own human dimension – and understanding.

Within 50 years of his passing, Dee's Enochian calls were being worked with in exclusive Magick circles throughout Europe – underground, exclusive, elite and often misused. The Golden Dawn, a pre-eminent Magickal society at the turn of the twentieth century worked with Enochian Magick to call upon Angels. This form of Magick is now available to almost anyone who wishes to explore its power.

Exile From the Court of the Virgin Queen

Soon the court was full of whispers – rumours about John Dee's obsession with necromancy, demon worship and outright sorcery. Dee's use of scandalous Magickal fervent methods – as well as the presence of Kelley – so close to the throne created strain in Dee's relationships with Elizabeth I. A practical ruler, Elizabeth was astute, sharp and clever enough to realise Dee's credibility was being undermined by his experiments and his choice of colleague. She slowly began to distance herself from Dee, unwilling to have her rule tainted by the suspicion of Witchcraft, a crime her Mother had been executed for. Dee's association with Kelley may have undermined his stature in the court, but he was too enthralled by the results the unlikely pair were getting to turn back.

His relationship with Kelley became obsessive, and he trusted Kelley's channelings absolutely – so much so that when Kelley suggested the pair move from England to Bohemia, where the energy would be better for their experiments, and where royal support was guaranteed, Dee agreed to abandon his beloved England. His family, his young wife, his brood of children were uprooted, taken from their lives of certainty and comfort, and into the unknown they went, led by a man who felt that with every session with Kelley, with every message and every secret being passed on, he was reaching a kind of climax to his Magickal destiny. Ultimately, Dee's desire to speak directly with God led to a series of amazing experiments that lasted for years, and took the pair far from England and across the world in search of the secrets of the language of Angels.

How Did Dee and Kelley Do Their Work?

If you are ever fortunate enough to visit the magnificent and haunting British Museum in London, be sure to head to a small chamber known as the Enlightenment Room. Near the back of that room, in a small cabinet, you can see for yourself some of the most renowned Magickal tools in existence, including the infamous 'smoking mirror' – or obsidian mirror Dee first began to scry with.

This small, dark oval mirror is entirely made of obsidian, or volcanic glass, and appears to 'smoke' from within, a kind of visual reference to the volcano it originates from. No doubt it was also considered a portal to the fires of hell itself by some of the Elizabethans who beheld it. We know it was created in Mexico, and was most likely a gift from Elizabeth to her pre-eminent magician. Was this the mirror that Kelley began to use so effectively to connect with what he described as Angels, and which allowed him to see into the future of Dee and the luminaries of Europe who sought out their bizarre counsel?

The Magickal Mirror of Dr Dee

Dr Dee's obsidian mirror is a great Magickal artefact, one which we are able to view in the British Museum today. It was brought to England by the Spanish, perhaps the Spanish ambassadors, after the Cortes expeditions between 1527 and 1530, and most likely presented as a gift to Elizabeth I, who then passed it on to her Wizard. This mirror was said to literally have belonged to the Meso-American deity Tezcatlipoca, whose domain was Magick, warriors and rulers – a God to whom the rulers of the Americas would turn to for guidance on the outcome of their every decision. Dee, working for Elizabeth, scried over and over with crystals, but it was this mirror that he became fascinated with, and it became one of his most treasured possessions. Ultimately, though, it was Edward Kelley who received

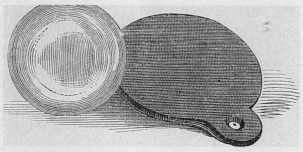

'The Smoking Mirror'

the sought-after visions from what became known as the Smoking Mirror.

Q: What is obsidian?

A: Obsidian forms when volcanic lava cools. It is a perfect surface upon which to scry as it is extremely reflective, yet dark and mysterious, and a completely 'alchemical' material.

Q: What is scrying?

A: Scrying is the art of 'seeing' the future in an object by entering a form of trance. The most usual form of scrying is within a black mirror, or within a crystal ball, both of which Dee and Kelley used frequently.

Within the cabinet are several other curiosities – humble enough to look at, but humming with unseen power. One is the pair's scrying crystal, known as the Apport of Uriel (an apport is a physical object that appears during séance, mediumship or spiritual trance sessions). This dark golden egg-shaped crystal was said to materialise during a channeling session, having being held out to Dee by an Angel – none other than the Angel Uriel.

There are also several wax tablets containing complex sigils, including the amazing Sigil of Ameth (Hebrew for 'truth'). The messages from the Angels would come through in another language, one of symbols and signs, which eventually formed an entire system of Magick, of invocations and channelings from various messengers of God. Dee painstakingly inscribed these onto altar cloths, wax tablets as altar items, and wrote down the words with which humans could open up the worlds and call upon the Angels themselves – in their own language. This system of Magick is more in use today than at any other time in history, with charismatic occultists like Aleister Crowley using Dee's own invocations to connect with the Angels and to speak directly with the Divine.

'Sigil of Ameth'

Magickal Practicum –
How to scry like John Dee and Edward Kelley

The word 'scry' has its roots in the old Anglo Saxon word *descry* meaning to reveal, or to see. It is also the root of our modern word 'describe' … when we scry, we are releasing the hold our conscious mind has over our abilities to see, and allowing the element we are working with to share its wisdom and insights into our question.

It is most often performed with a semi-reflective surface. To scry like Edward Kelley and John Dee, you will need a crystal ball or a dark mirror. You may also wish to cover a mirror with a dark transparent fabric to achieve the feel of Dee's legendary obsidian Smoking Mirror.

Find a quiet space. Make it atmospheric – burn candles, turn down harsh lighting, turn off your phones and electronic devices and play some music that has no lyrics, just restful, blissful sound. Sit down in front of your scrying mirror, or crystal ball, or hold it in front of you. Close your eyes and take three deep breaths. Keep breathing steadily and gently open your eyes and soften your gaze: Let your eyes fall upon the mirror or crystal ball. Don't look at what it appears to be … let it be simply a shape, a tool, a door through which you can see. See into it ... see the worlds within it ... slow everything down ... feel the pulse of life moving throughout your body, and your energy field ... and softening your gaze ... allowing your eyesight to soften, even blur a little ... and shift.

While gazing into the mirror or the crystal ball, ask your questions. Be patient and allow patterns to form, and feel yourself enter a trance-like state. You may see shapes or patterns, or even hear voices. Remain calm, soft, open to receiving ... and when you feel you have enough information, or have done enough work for now, gently allow your eyes to close, take three deep breaths to break the scrying spell, and then open your eyes.

Write down what you may have received – it is easy to forget the details within even minutes of this practice, so get what you can in writing as fast as you can, just like John Dee. When you have finished, blow out the candles, turn off the music, and change the atmosphere back to that of ordinary reality.

Congratulations! You have just scried. Of course, this is a craft that will take much practice to master (although it can come naturally and swiftly to some!). You are on your way to working Magick like the Wizard of the Burning Times!

An Elizabethan Sex Scandal

The relationship between the genius and the channeler
lasted until Kelley persuaded Dee to sleep with his wife,
Joanna – and to permit Kelley to sleep with Dee's own
young, very beautiful and extremely fertile wife, Jane.
It is clear from Dee's journals that this last, volatile
experiment went ahead, and Jane Dee also wrote of

her struggle to comply with Kelley's directive – and it
is clear she did not relish the task her husband and his
co-conspirator persuaded her to fulfill: 'I trust that though
I give myself thus to be used, that God would turn me
into a stone before he would suffer me in my obedience
to receive any shame or inconvenience,' she wrote in her
journal. Despite Jane's reluctant compliance, this bizarre
arrangement ultimately destroyed the relationship
between Dee and the channeler, eroding trust, causing
bitterness, growing resentment and deep regret on the
part of the deeply pious Dee, who loved his wife
passionately. Jane bore a child after this experiment,
and Dee never knew if the last child to bear his name
was his own or Kelley's. As Kelley had no children, he
offered to take the child off their hands, and it seemed
that, truly, that was what he had wanted all along, with
Jane serving unwittingly as his way to fulfill that ambition.
This was the last time Dee would risk his family, his
reputation and his safety for the sake of working with
Kelley's own twisted brand of genius. The pair parted
ways, perhaps Dee finally realising that an Angel would
never have sent such a message, even through Kelley,
whom he had relied upon and trusted so completely for
so many years. The pair separated and Dee gained
employment casting horoscopes, advising dignitaries,
and quietly putting about the word that he was ready

to return home to England, if his Queen would but welcome him once again.

Life After Kelley

After word of Dee's break with Kelley made its way back to the English Court, the Wizard was finally called back to Britain by Elizabeth I. While this would have seemed a great sign, Dee's fortunes, health and family never quite recovered from those years in exile. Upon returning to the family home at Mortlake, he discovered that his beloved estate had been pillaged over and over during his absence. The proud house and its green lands were neglected, and there were ugly, deep holes gouged into the ground by the hundreds of fortune hunters who had taken advantage of the doctor's absence to search out his rumoured buried treasure. In his precious library the family discovered that Dee's own papers had been burned, his valuable rare grimoires and Arabic treasures of mathematics and medicine had been stolen, and the books of Magick that remained were torn, damaged and flung to the dust-laden floor. What a sight to welcome the once proud Merlin of Mortlake home! This broke the heart of the great Wizard – years of collecting, years of caring for his treasure, the knowledge within his library, treated with contempt. The culprits were never found, but the suspects were many. Dee's writings and collection

were rumoured to have earned him his millions, and the
favour of the Angels – and his treasure maps were highly
sought after. In the wake of this destruction, Elizabeth
took pity on her former adviser, and Dee was granted a
life pension by the Queen, who had always retained great
affection and respect for her Merlin, even if this could not
be overtly displayed. He was given the position of Warden
of Christ's College, Manchester, in 1595. He was grateful,
but he yearned to be in his library near London, at home,
with his books, near his Queen, and with his beloved family
including Jane, who had done so much for him and had
remained loyal and in love throughout their entire marriage.
Effectively, this was a kind of banishment – and a subtle
punishment – a role which was profoundly unsuited to
this Wizard.

While he was in Manchester, the plague cut a swathe
through London and its surrounds, and took in its dreadful
wake his wife and four of his eight children. Night fell upon
the old man, and he struggled to recover from the volley of
losses that had befallen his personal and professional life.

The times did not favour Dee. He returned to London
after Elizabeth's death and found that the new King,
James, was fixated on wiping out anything that resembled
Witchcraft or sorcery. Dee's pension was withdrawn, and
he resorted to selling off what was left of his collection to
support himself and his daughter, who cared for him as he

grew old and frail and allowed himself to fade from the public view, hoping to also spare his daughter any accusations of Witchcraft. Finally, Dee took his records of Angelic communications and the old man dug deep into the existing holes that the treasure hunters had made so many years ago when he returned to England. He and his daughter dragged the chest, heavy with manuscripts, to the grounds, and buried it deep underground knowing that his years of research and his life's work might remain secret for the time being. Feeling almost safe, after living most of his life with the threat of execution or exile, Dee lived simply and died quietly in 1609 having been on the planet for eighty-two amazing years. He might have kept much of his work discreet – but fate would have it otherwise.

A Magickal Discovery

In 1659, a discovery was made in the grounds of Dee's home. A chest was dug up, containing Dee's journals of Angelic calls, invocations and journals of Magick, pages from grimoires and personal notes were brought back from the dead. They were published that same year, and sensationalised as the journals of a sorcerer dabbling with demonic communication. Within the chest were paintings of Dee – which is how we came to know that he is the very archetype of the Wizard: tall and slender, wearing dark robes and with a long, flowing grey beard and piercing, obsessive brown eyes. Here we have the figure who inspired the fascination with Merlin, Gandalf; almost every creation of any Wizard since owes something to one of the greatest Wizards of them all – Doctor John Dee.

THE LEGEND OF SALEM:

"THE REV. GEORGE BURROUGHS WAS ACCUSED OF WITCHCRAFT ON THE EVIDENCE OF FEATS OF STRENGTH, TRIED, HUNG, AND BURIED BENEATH THE GALLOWS."

Salem: A Page from the Devil's History Book

HOW THE DISCOVERY OF WITCHES CREATED CHAOS IN NEW ENGLAND

1692

❧

'The Magistrates, Ministers, Jewries, and all the People in general, being so much inraged and incensed against us by the Delusion of the Devil, which we can term no other, by reason we know in our own Consciences, we are all Innocent Persons.'

John Procter, July 23, 1692.
Written prior to his execution by hanging.

FOUR-YEAR-OLD Dorothy Good was homeless, dirty and cold. Very, very cold. Spring was late that year in 1692 in Salem Village, and she had grown weak with the hunger and the coughing and the begging. Spring would be along soon, her mother told her, over and over, and then there would be food to eat and people's hearts would grow a little kinder. In Spring they might find some work in the fields, and a barn to shelter under. But it was already March, and the bitter winds still blew the dirty snow along the streets, and even the kindest people of Salem had grown hard.

⌒∾⌒

Dorothy Good and her mother, Sarah, were outsiders in the Puritan stronghold of Salem, a tiny village in the God-fearing colony of Massachusetts. There Sarah and Dorothy scrounged a living in a world made harsh by threat of Indian attack, bitter cold, and the strict codes of New England puritanism. Every Sunday for years, Dorothy had stretched out her cold hands towards the Goodwives and Goodmen departing one of the three-hour church services everyone attended twice on Sunday. Sometimes people would take pity on them, and pass on coins, or some bread, especially if the service had encouraged charity and compassion.

But then Reverend Parris came to town. He did not like the Good women loitering out the front of his church, mingling with his congregation. Not Sarah Good with her outspoken ways and her belly swelling with another pregnancy, nor her unkempt child who barely knew her Bible. The new Reverend was unstinting in reprimanding those who offered money to the beggar women, and times had grown tough.

The extended winter wasn't just hurting the Goods. Spring's lateness was making the people of both Salem

Village and Salem Town uneasy. The unseasonal weather had the potential to ruin their harvests and cause their animals to get sick, and on Sundays between services people huddled in cold groups and wondered aloud at what had brought their ill fortune. People began to hoard resources – starvation was a real prospect in the New World, and bread on the table was a sign of favour from God. Freezing weather, long after Spring was due, was a sign that something was very wrong in Salem.

And then the talk outside church began to change. Betty Parris and Abigail Williams were said to be bewitched.

Reverend Parris's own household was infected by the Devil.

A Devil's Shield Against a Devil's Sword

Although Salem was a very devout Christian village, there were plenty of people within the colonies who practised folk Magick and healing. For hundreds of years, Christianity and folk Magick had lived side by side – until the changes brought about by the reign of James I made the practice of the old ways punishable by death. Even so, folk Magick and healing did not die out – the two were often intertwined, and just where the line could be drawn was difficult to say.

One of the men imprisoned for Witchcraft during the Salem trials was Roger Toohaker, a healer who had a small farm just outside of the village. He had claimed for many years he had charms that would work against the powers of Witches.

He had taught his wife Mary and his daughter the old charms and folk remedies, which ultimately led to their imprisonment.

He claimed that his daughter had killed a Witch by boiling her urine in a cauldron over the stove, with some nails and pins thrown into the brew for good measure.

Roger passed away in prison awaiting trial, but his wife and daughter survived, as does their charm for killing a Witch.

This kind of work really did test the boundaries between healing and Magick, and Cotton Mather, the New England Minister who tirelessly supported the trials and executions in Salem, claimed that doing such work was using 'the Devil's shield against the Devil's sword.'

March 1692 – The Devil Comes to Town

Betty Parris was eight years old and her cousin, Abigail Williams, was eleven. In late February, the two girls had

begun to behave in strange ways. They contorted their
bodies into bizarre shapes, tore at their clothes, their
tongues protruded and they screamed and wailed. They
walked on all fours and cried out they were being hurt,
and then would lie, totally still, as though asleep with
eyes open.

The Reverend Parris called a doctor, William Griggs,
to examine the girls. Griggs was baffled, and alarmed.
There was no natural cause he could find for the girls'
afflictions, and so he could only conclude that the cause
of their suffering was supernatural.

Parris, fearing the backlash from an already uneasy
congregation, called in John Hale, a reverend of nearby
Beverly. This man had seen cases of actual Witchcraft,
and Parris trusted his judgement. After seeing the girls
Hale decided that Doctor Griggs had been right.
The girls were bewitched. The Devil, he declared, had
come to Salem.

Dorothy Good probably didn't pay a great deal of
attention to such talk. She was most likely concerned
with the gnawing pains of hunger in her stomach, and
where she and her mother would sleep that night, and
what to name her new baby brother or sister.

But all of Salem Village and Salem Town would soon
become obsessed. Worse still, the bizarre behaviour of
Abigail and Betty seemed to be spreading. Other young

women began to scream and claw their faces, crying out
that they were being pinched, pricked and choked by the
Devil, a tall black man, a winged creature, a faceless demon.
Abigail and Betty were questioned, and it was demanded
that they reveal who had bewitched them. Leading question
after leading question followed, until Abigail Williams,
fearful that she would be accused of witching Betty Parris,
flung the first of the accusations: It was Tituba Indian, she
cried, pointing to the Parris's slave, a woman who had been
with the family from their time on the sugar plantations
in Barbados.

The Accused

It was Tituba, Abigail claimed, who came to them and
stopped them breathing, pressing down on them. It was
Tituba who knew the ways of the Devil and who was his
creature, it was Tituba who caused them to scream and cry
and scratch at their arms and legs. And, most damningly, it
was Tituba who had made a Witch cake.

Tituba was taken by the Reverend Parris and John Hale,
and beaten until her cries of innocence were replaced with
weeping admission of guilt. Yes, I am the witch, she said.
Yes, I asked the girls the write in the Devil's book. But, she
said, I was tortured until I would do his will. Others had
sent the Devil to her.

Tituba and the Witch Cake

When Betty Parris and Abigail Williams took suddenly, strangely ill, crawling about on all fours and screaming in their sleep, Reverend Parris called in the doctor, William Griggs, who thought the children bewitched. Tituba Indian thought she could help – and made a Witch cake to find out what was wrong with the children. Tituba took the urine of Betty and Abigail and cooked it in a cake of rye, and fed it to the dog on February 25th of 1692. It was believed that the dog's reaction would show who had bewitched the girls, and how much danger they were in. Tituba was not engaging in any remedy she had learned in Barbados – for it was a parishioner, Mary Sibley, who taught her how to make a Witch cake, and suggested its use for the girls. This Witch cake led to Tituba being accused of Witchcraft by the girls, who may have seen the cake being made with their urine and the dog being fed it. Regardless, it made Tituba an easy target. Mary Sibley was chastised publicly in Church by Reverend Parris for this act. She apologised, and no more was said of the Witch cake to her. Its making, however, was used as evidence of Witchcraft against Tituba.

So, John Hale watched Reverend Parris flog Tituba until she told them who had made her an instrument of the Devil. 'Names, names,' they cried, desperate to save her soul. And finally she said, 'It was Sarah Good, sir, who choked me and told me to obey the Devil, or suffer this torment.' It had been Sarah Good, the beggar woman, who was a Witch, sir.

And as the name of Sarah Good was spoken, the girls cried out in agreement. The magistrate demanded more names, and Tituba added others, pressed as she was by the whip to deliver name upon name upon name. With every name, the girls, led by Abigail, twitched and shook and fell to the floor, crying out, and as every accusation was made they cried out that yes, yes, that was the Witch.

And so Tituba was imprisoned, as was Sarah Osborne, and Sarah Good. Pregnant and poor, with none to speak for her, she was shackled in a dank cell, and little Dorothy Good was left to the streets.

Tituba had confessed, and things became easier for her afterwards. And as the names of the accused piled high, others did the same. But Sarah Good would not confess, and the others then claimed that her daughter, Dorothy, that dirty little beggar girl who did not know her Bible, had come to them in dreams and bit and scratched them while they lay abed. She was questioned by magistrates for three days.

Practical Magick –
'Be Silent' Spell Bottle

Perhaps if Tituba had used this remedy to stop Abigail and Betty accusing so many people of Witchcraft, hysteria would not have spread through Salem. But then again, should she have been discovered using it, perhaps the bottle itself may have sealed her fate. The old folk Magicks were still alive in Salem and the puritan village of New England. This spell, or form of folk Magick is based on the old practice of burying or hanging a bottle by the entrance to a house. The bottle was said to capture any curses or ill-wishes being sent into the home. This kind of folk charm is practised all over the world to this day, and has variations in many different cultures. This simple 'Bottle' spell is designed to capture unpleasant energy and to stop people's gossip or negative words about you. Let's hope you never have to use it.

You'll need:

A small bottle

Some pieces of hematite, osbidian onyx or smoky quartz crystal

How:

Imagine a circle of light all around you, focus and still your emotions, become very clear and calm, open your bottle and say:

Be silent
Be still
I wish you no ill
Into this your words of hate
Fall harmless and dissipate
They are gone, they do no harm
I move on, this is my charm

Say this three times OR three times three. Place a few pieces of hematite or obsidian or onyx or smoky quartz (all are very good and very protective, slightly different energies but similar qualities for the purpose of this spell) into the bottle. Keep the bottle open and place it at your door or an entrance to your house so it can catch anything nasty being sent your way. After three days, when the energy has been captured, stopper it up. If the energy starts again, open it up again, pop three pinches of salt inside it, and repeat the process.

The Reverend Deodat Lawson, an eyewitness and former minister, confirmed: 'The Magistrates and Ministers also did informe me, that they apprehended a child of Sarah G. and Examined it, being between 4 and 5 years of Age. And as to

matter of Fact, they did Unanimously affirm, that when this Child did but cast its eye upon the afflicted persons, they were tormented, and they held her Head, and yet so many as her eye could fix upon were afflicted.'

Dorothy was asked the usual questions. She was told her mother was a Witch; therefore she must be a Witch.

'On the 26th of March, Mr Hathorne, Mr Corwin and Mr Higison were at the Prison-Keepers house to examine the Child. The Child told them there, it had a little Snake that used to Suck on the lowest Joint of her Fore-Finger. When they inquired where, pointing to other places, the child told them, not there, but there, pointing on the Lowest point of the Fore-Finger; where they observed a deep Red Spot, about the Bigness of a Flea-bite.'

How to Test a Witch

In the New England colonies of the late seventeenth century, a person accused of the crime of practising Witchcraft would be questioned by the local reverend, or a doctor, and then by magistrates of the court. Accusations were all that was needed, and proof could include your neighbours being ill, the weather changing, people noticing you talk to yourself or, sin of sins, singing out loud or dancing. The questions asked were most often leading – how long have you been a Witch? When did you sign the Devil's book? What has the Devil promised you? Often, random sections of the Bible were quoted, and if the accused could not name the section or complete the quote, this lack of biblical knowledge was assumed to be evidence of guilt. If the person did not pass this trial, which could last for hours, and continue for days, while imprisoned, the next step was a physical examination.

It was widely considered that the Devil, the Devil's evil spirits, and/or the familiars in league with a Witch, suckled from a Witch's teat. This could be a mole, or a skin tag, or a third nipple, but all of these physical attributes were considered to be evidence of having the Devil's teat. If anyone had a skin tag or a mole, which changed colour or appearance, or came and went, that was considered to be absolutely the Devil's teat.

There was a third method that could be used to test a Witch – Witch ducking, or the floating test.

In 1706 in New England, Luke Hill charged Grace Sherwood with Witchcraft. Examiners found two marks upon her body, and during her trial the judges decided to have Sherwood put to a trial by water. On July 10, 1706, Grace Sherwood was tied about the waist by a thick rope and two men took either end of the rope, one on each side of a pond. Sherwood was dragged into the pond and somehow managed to stay alive – or, as the court put it, she floated – and thus she was determined to be a Witch, and sentenced to death. Sherwood was subjected to the test twice during her trial, and it is not known what her ultimate fate was.

Beggar Girl in Chains

And so, because of this flea-bite, and what a four-year-old girl said to three grown men, by the time Spring finally arrived in the colony, both Sarah Good and her daughter finally had a roof over their head. A special set of chains had to be cast and made for the little beggar girl, and Sarah

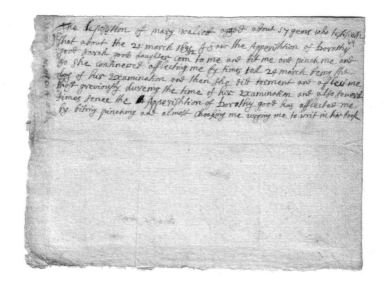

gave birth in the prison over Summer. By that time, Bridget
Bishop had been hung – believed to be a Witch – and
more were to follow. Sarah Good, Rebecca Nurse (a healer),
Elizabeth Howe, Susannah Martin and Sarah Wilds were
all hung for the crime of being Witches on July 19. Under
the high Summer sun Sarah Good stood at the gallows,
refusing to confess, desperate with fear for her newborn,
Mercy, and her little one, Dorothy. She was defiant to the
end, blazing with anger and dignity.

'You are a liar,' she cried out to Reverend Parris, to the
girls shaking and trembling, still calling her Witch from

the base of the gallows. To Cotton Mather, the powerful Minister lurking at the back of the crowd on horseback, she said, 'I am no more a Witch than you are a Wizard, and if you take away my life God will give you blood to drink.'

Others refused to admit they were in league with the Devil, and so, throughout that Summer and into the Fall of 1692, nineteen women in total were hung as Witches, as well as farmers, a reverend, healers and others who had done no harm. Old Giles Carey refused to speak at all, so was pressed to death by having boulders heaped upon him till he died. And Mercy Good, in the care of Dorothy who was just five and in prison, passed away not long after her mother's execution.

Dorothy was in chains for nine months, from March 24, 1692, until December 10, 1692, when someone paid her bail of fifty pounds – a fortune in that day. We know she was officially deemed insane – though today we might call it post-traumatic stress disorder. She wasn't the only child accused of Witchcraft during the Witch-hunts of Salem. Eight other children under the age of twelve were accused and imprisoned – and every one of them was the child of a supposed Witch. By the time the hysteria had run its course, over 200 people were imprisoned and awaiting trial.

When one governor's own wife was accused of Witchcraft, sober heads and powerful people began to say that enough was enough. Even Cotton Mather backed down from his demands that all of the Devil's creatures must be found out and destroyed. By the Winter of that year, the accused began to be released back into the communities that had muddied their names, stolen their freedom, ruined their trades and very nearly taken their lives.

Freedom was no simple thing. Release was conditional on bail, and bail was expensive. Tituba, who had remained imprisoned from the time of her confession, stayed locked up longer than most. She had earned the wrath of Reverend Parris, her legal owner and the only person who could free her, by recanting her own confession and testimony while in prison. She was purchased, finally, for the sum of seven pounds, after thirteen months in prison, and released into what passed as freedom for one who was a slave.

Thou Shalt Not Suffer a Witch to Live

In 1542 a law was passed by the English parliament that made Witchcraft a 'felony punishable by death and forfeiture of goods and chattels.' Now, that last part is very important. Not only did you lose your life when convicted as a Witch – but your property could not go to your children or heirs – it became the King's, or the local government's. This underpinned so many cases that were to come – and some believe that the early New England cases were almost always driven by avaricious neighbours coveting the property and houses of others. Single women of means without children and who refused marriage offers were particularly vulnerable to such accusations – their property was seen as easy pickings.

In 1597, James VI of Scotland – who would become James I of England after the death of Elizabeth I – wrote and published a book called *Daemonologie*. In it he made the claim that Witchcraft flourished most in the 'wild partes of the world.' That was taken to mean the colonies, the countryside, the places where there were less churches, more pagans. The colonies were already viewed with suspicion. In order to lessen their taxes and reduce interference, the colonies were keen to adopt these laws and prove how Godfearing a place the new lands could become. In 1604, parliament passed an 'acte against conjuration, witchcrafte and dealing with evill and wicked spirits.' For the first time, the colonies were formally given the power to prosecute accused Witches.

James I is perhaps the person we can most single out to blame for the death of thousands of men, women and animals throughout the Witch hunts of Britain, and the Witch hunts of Germany, France and, eventually, the American colonies.

Not only did he pass laws making Witchcraft a crime punishable by death, he introduced an English translation of the Bible during his reign. In this bible was the order, 'Thou shalt not suffer a witch to live' – attributed to the Book of Exodus 22:18.

This was the first time this sentence had ever appeared in any bible, and it was soon to become one of the most quoted parts of the Christian book. This sentence was not in any original biblical work, and was a deliberate mistranslation of Hebrew words. James I did this in order to pursue his fascination with the torture and punishment and ultimate death of women (and men and children and animals) who were practising what he considered to be the 'dark arts'.

The original biblical passage does not mention anything about Witches at all. Instead, the line contains the word *chasaph*, which most accurately translates to 'poisoner', or 'a murderer who uses poison'. Witches had nothing to do with this statement – until James I changed it to suit his own purposes.

This was protested against in his own time, by the daemonology author Rigenald Scott in his book *The Discoverie of Witchcraft*. Scott bravely pointed out that the word had been incorrectly translated and that the text had always referred to poison. In rebuke, James I ordered that all of Scott's works be purchased and burned.

'Thou shalt not suffer a witch to live,' became an accepted part of the Bible, considered to be the word of God, and this sentence went on to be mistranslated into the Lutheran Bible in Germany, and a French translation followed suit. The biblical evidence to put Witches to death soon spread around the Christian world – and, ultimately, to New England. The words were quoted again and again in Salem.

If it had not been for this deliberate change of the Bible, many a good woman and man would not have been hung, or burned; many a child would not have been imprisoned; and many an animal would not have been cruelly murdered.

Recognition of Innocence

In 1711, nearly twenty years after Salem's crazed Spring and Summer of 1692, compensation was offered to many of the families involved. Names were cleared, informally, and yet families did not come forward to accept the compensation or the implied exoneration. It was pride, a show of too little, too late, and fear that kept them far away from the magistrates' rooms. After all, John Hale had published *A Modest Enquiry into the Nature of Witchcraft* in 1705 – a modest enquiry, which seemed to validate the trials and its methods, even while he cautiously condemned the use of spectral evidence. Perhaps it was just too soon. As late as 1957 Ann Pudeator's name was cleared, as well as other people who had been accused.

In 1992, a memorial was created in Salem, which features the words of the accused, carved into stone. And in 2001, more than three hundred years after their execution, five more victims were officially exonerated by the state of Massachusetts.

The act, signed in public at Halloween, was witnessed by the descendants of Bridget Bishop, Alice Parker, Wilmott Red, Margaret Scott and Susannah Martin, and cheered by three thousand onlookers.

It is not known if Sarah Good or Dorothy Good were among those unnamed persons who were cleared. Perhaps they have no descendants to fight for their name.

❧

Salem was no lone incident. Women and men and animals alike were convicted as Witches and had been hung in Virginia, on ships on their way to the colonies, and in towns across the colonies. Reputable single women with land were vulnerable to accusations, and anyone with a tavern, or who sang, or enjoyed sex, or who was a healer, or married to one, or was sharp, outspoken or disliked, or doing well financially was also likely to be accused. The trials were often swift, and

punishment was death. The puritan colonies were made up of exiled Calvinists, the protestant branch that took most literally the mistranslated words of the King James Bible – thou shalt not suffer a Witch to live.

Sympathy for the Devil

Painter, climber, poet, spy: Aleister Crowley, the Wickedest Man in the World

1875–1947

❧

'I have been accused of being a "black magician". No more foolish statement was ever made about me. I despise the thing to such an extent that I can hardly believe in the existence of people so debased and idiotic as to practice it.' [sic]

Aleister Crowley

A YOUNG WOMAN is walking through the darkening streets of Soho, London, her violin case swinging by her side with every stride. She is late and she is in a hurry and she is nervous, but her head is held high, because she has an appointment to meet the man who she knows can change her life, and she has heard he cannot abide cowardice. A man she knows can help her break through every shred of artifice and unnatural conditioning she possesses, a man who can help her recognise the true force of her great talent and become the artist she knows she was

 meant to be. She reaches her destination – a small bookshop with an overstuffed armchair in one of the corners, and pushes the door open, ready to meet her destiny.

And there, his jowled face heavy from years of debauchery, tall, with a great grand gesture and surprising elegance, he stands, and bows to her.

'My lady,' he says, and guides her to the seat next to his. 'Play for me.'

⤜⤛

Who knows if this is the way the great and very young Australian violinist Leila Waddell became one of Aleister Crowley's Scarlet Women. What we do know is that their meeting led to her taking part in the Rites of Artemis, followed by the Rites of Eleusis, a series of staged rituals starring Crowley and Waddell performing re-imagined rites of ancient Greece on the stage for jaded Londoners desperate to be shocked out of their Victorian haze – and to take money off the hands of bored gentlemen and women. It was a sensation.

For that was, perhaps, what this great magician and dissolute man represented – a sensation. The human storm of decadence and irreverence and utter rebellion that was

Aleister Crowley finally tore off the lid of repression from the Victorian era he had been born into, opening up a world ravaged by wars, the deaths of too many young men, a time when people were instructed in every facet of human behaviour: how to dress, the right way to hold a teacup, and the people one ought to marry.

This man, this Beast, was the antidote, albeit the sometimes foul one, to an age of utter imprisonment of the senses. For to understand anything of Aleister Crowley is to understand the era into which he was born.

No Ordinary Man

The man who so scandalised the world and charmed young Leila Waddell was born at the height of the Victorian era, a time when piano legs were covered should they inspire

lusty thoughts in the men and women who gazed upon
them; in the time when the theories of Freud and Jung were
percolating; and when the utter repression resulted, perhaps,
in the disgusting excesses of the first world war.

Aleister Crowley (pronounced, his preference, to rhyme
with Holy) was born in 1875 and named Edward Alexander
Crowley. His father, a rich brewer, whose company had
a series of ales – Crowley ales in every tavern – was also,
strangely, a leader of the Plymouth Brethren, a peculiar and
mysterious radical Protestant sect. In the Crowley household
there was no Christmas, no birthdays were celebrated, and
the scriptures were read morning and evening. And young
Edward drank it all in. He adored his father, who took his
son on his missions, persuading people to the way of the
Brethren, convincing them that they needed no pastor, no
priest ... only the word of God, and a strict and pure life.

Edward was doted on by his father, a charismatic and
intelligent man, but his mother, oh, his mother! His mother
found him lacking in too many ways, sensing in his
passionate and charismatic nature and fierce will a man
who would ultimately go his own way – instead of that of
God. And so this young man preached with his father and
was punished by his mother. Until...

At fourteen, young Crowley had sex for the first time,
upon, he claimed, his own parents' bed, with a maid. Spoiled
and over-disciplined, willful, religious and with a flame now
lit within him by the great joy of physical union, he began

to link this love of religion and this burning brightness of sexual ecstasy into one gargantuan vision. Through the act of sex he had come closer to what he felt might be the real God – not any God he had previously learned about at any lecture,  or during any prayer reading. He knew he was to be like his father – but the message he would share was to be his own.

Perhaps things would have been very different for the man who grew to be called the Wickedest Man in the World if his father had lived. But he did not, and when his father died of tongue cancer in 1887, the representative of God within his home became his mother. And their battle for her son's soul began in earnest.

The Birth of the Beast

Discovering his love for masturbation, orgasm and the bedding of maids, his mother called 12-year-old Edward the 'Beast'. Edward did not deny this new name, but

 hugged it tight because defining himself by anything his mother hated was becoming one of his favourite pastimes.

It was as if the first electric light had been switched on. The Beast! He gathered the name to himself, and suddenly knew his own nature. He was more, he knew, Lucifer than Saint, and could never stop desiring the connection to ecstasy he had found through the union of the flesh.

He left home, his mother relieved to be sending him to Cambridge, where she was sure, no doubt, that her beastly son would be disciplined, shaped back into the man she wanted him to be.

But the will within the boy was strong, and his intelligence was fierce, and his desire to be his own Self had been awakened. Religion. Sex. Intellect. Crowley's path as a complete non-conformist, a profligate rebel and one of Magick's most advanced thinkers was set.

He changed his name to Aleister.

'Edward did not seem to suit me and the diminutives Ted or Ned were even less appropriate. Alexander was too long and Sandy suggested tow hair and freckles. I had read in some book or other that the most favourable name for becoming famous was one consisting of a dactyl followed by a spondee,

as at the end of a hexameter: like Jeremy Taylor. Aleister
Crowley fulfilled these conditions and Aleister is the Gaelic
form of Alexander. To adopt it would satisfy my romantic
ideals. The atrocious spelling A-L-E-I-S-T-E-R was
suggested as the correct form by Cousin Gregor, who ought
to have known better. In any case, A-L-A-I-S-D-A-I-R
makes a very bad dactyl. For these reasons I saddled myself
with my present nom-de-guerre – I can't say that I feel sure
that I facilitated the process of becoming famous. I should
doubtless have done so, whatever name I had chosen.'

So Edward was dead. And Aleister was born.

Newborn Aleister dressed outrageously, played chess
brilliantly, rampaged his way
through the bordellos of
Cambridge and wrote
poetry instead of studying.
An outstanding athlete, he
climbed mountains through
the fog of ferocious hangovers.
He contracted gonorrhea,
bested a World Chess
Champion, and set out to drink
more, fornicate more, live more

than any human being ought. He read widely, and well,
and studied just enough to stay at the esteemed college his
mother had so foolishly felt he was safe at. He was hypnotic

in personality, disturbingly amoral and utterly sure of himself. He experimented sexually and dedicated himself to pleasure.

In the Britain of these times, bisexuality was considered perversion, sex between males punishable by prison. Crowley didn't seem to care. He had made his own experience of life his religion – and he tore through lovers, through life, like a starving man tears meat off a bone.

How to Break all the Right Rules

Crowley matriculated from Cambridge in the northern Autumn of 1895 and undertook training for the British secret service in St Petersburg – his role as a spy and secret agent has been well documented. During this time, his mountain climbing became a passionate vocation. Those who love to paint Crowley as a dark figure – which he would have encouraged – have often claimed he was a pro-Nazi sympathiser, but it has since been proved that Crowley was given a mission by the British to serve as a German propagandist to gain access to their secrets. He had, in his pockets on his deathbed, letters from the director of naval intelligence – perhaps knowing this was his only sure way of setting the record straight once he had passed.

Crowley never did care much for reputation. When his mother passed away, and with his only sibling, a sister, having died as a child, Crowley inherited a fortune. Not enough to call himself outrageously rich, but rich enough so that his life could become his own masterwork. The idea of being a middle-class brewer held no enticement at all. His life would be his invention and his masterpiece. In 1897 he began in earnest using the vast freedoms riches can afford. He focussed fiercely on his esoteric studies, ascending through the grades of Freemasonry, reading MacGregor Mathers and A.E. Waite, who had formed a secret society called the Hermetic Order of the Golden Dawn, and climbing and travelling. One of his most intense mystical experiences took place after ascending the Moench, a formidable mountain in Germany.

'I was awakened to the knowledge that I possessed a magical means of becoming conscious of and satisfying a part of my nature which had up to that moment concealed itself from me. It was an experience of horror and pain, combined with a certain ghostly terror, yet at the same time it was the key to the purest and holiest spiritual ecstasy that exists.'

Witch Wars: Crowley vs Mathers

Was Aleister Crowley under a curse unleashed by the Golden Dawn's MacGregor Mathers? With both his first wife, Rose, and then his second wife, Maria, ending their days in institutions, the death of his daughter, his lover's deaths of cancer and the loss of his fortune, Crowley certainly had reason to believe there were dark forces moving against him. The one most often cited as the wielder of the curse against Crowley was MacGregor Mathers.

The legend begins thus: Aleister Crowley was at home at Boleskin when his dogs began barking and howling. Minutes later they suddenly stopped. When Crowley went to investigate, his hounds were, inexplicably, dead, silenced, he believed, by MacGregor Mathers, Crowley's Magickal rival, his former teacher, and once dear friend. Crowley believed Mathers was hell-bent on destroying him and his new occult organisation in an all-out psychic blitzkrieg. Now, this tale is so woven into Magickal lore that when it comes to the truth, who knows? Perhaps the dogs were poisoned. They could have been ill and died far more slowly than Crowley claimed; but whatever the truth, there is no doubt that this gave Crowley the chance to charge his rival MacGregor Mathers with psychic attack. Before he could retaliate, Mathers was accused of sending a beautiful daemon after Crowley, who counterclaimed he turned her into a hag. Mathers, then, it was said, hypnotised a servant into attacking Crowley's wife, Rose, who was so affected she never recovered, and ended her years in an institution.

The incredible animosity between the two men affected their families and their own health – perhaps even that of the world. Ultimately, Crowley dealt a ritual Magickal death blow, calling up a demon to crush Mathers. Even the master magician could not contain the demon, and it is still said to be working its evil in the world today.

Climbing, sex, pushing himself to his very limits were becoming Crowley's trademarks – and made him a compelling free spirit who drew people to him.

Crowley revelled in being notorious as it gave claim that he was indeed the Beast from the Bible's Book of Revelation. Though not a joiner by nature, it was during this time that Crowley was introduced to the elite members of the Hermetic Order of the Golden Dawn, and at the turn of the century he was initiated into its highest ranks by MacGregor Mathers in Paris. The membership of Crowley in the ranks of this elite society created incredible turmoil: much of which Crowley delighted in, as he was nothing if not a provocateur. Scandalous as he was, he was driven to quest for the mystic – undertaking silent days of meditation, travelling to Mexico to work with shamans and take Peyote long before Jim Morrison of The Doors, and visiting Burma to practise yoga, which he eventually wrote a series of witty and engaging essays about, and which may, in effect, have introduced yoga to the Western world. He even managed to attempt to climb K2, or Chogori in the Himalayas, an expedition that was abandoned due to bad weather, and during which Crowley suffered snow-blindness and severe altitude sickness. Not for the last time, he was fortunate to make it down from the mountain.

When the Will Becomes the Law

Perhaps this brush with death led to what took place next. In 1903, Aleister met a woman who was the sister of a close friend, Gerald Kelly, and they married. Rose Crowley was a libertine like her husband, utterly devoted to him and to their Magick, and dedicated to the pursuit of their individual liberties and full self-expression. They embarked on an incredible honeymoon, sailing to Cairo and settling in that city. On one of their expeditions to the great pyramids, Aleister invoked the God Horus from the darkness within the tomb. Rose stopped him. She had entered a profound trance. Seeing what was happening, Crowley took paper and pen and began to write down what she was saying. In essence: 'They are waiting for you. They are here,' she said, over and over, swooning.

Within a month, much of what was to eventually become the Book of the Law had been delivered to Crowley, partly through Rose, via this connection with the ancient deities. Crowley's belief in himself and his Magick soared. He was now a part of the lineage of Egyptian Magick – the one the Gods called to, a part of the song of the ancients.

Practical Magick – Protect Yourself from a Crowley Curse

There is no doubt that Crowley and many other nineteenth century magicians often hexed and cursed each other. The secret nature of these groups was fiercely protected from the outside world, and internal alliances were formed, then shattered with startling ease, sometimes leading to Magickal vendettas that lasted beyond the lifetime of the curse-bringer. One member of the Golden Dawn that Crowley may have learned from was Dion Fortune, whose book *Psychic Self-Defense* is still a classic. She was the moral fibre of that group and unlike Crowley in almost every way except for their love of Magick, their intelligence and their talent.

It is unlikely you will ever draw the ire of a powerful magician like MacGregor Mathers. But all of us need to know the basics of psychic self-defence and protection. Here are some simple ways to protect yourself from curses and psychic attack:

- Read Dion Fortune's book *Psychic Self-Defense*.
- Use the stones Black Tourmaline, black onyx or black obsidian – carrying them in your handbag, or placing them under your pillow to prevent psychic invasion while you sleep.
- Deconstruct your fears. Understand why they trigger your anxiety. Work with friends, or a qualified empathetic counsellor to help reduce the fear you feel.
- Cloak yourself, head to toe with not a single gap, with loving, protective Light.
- Feel your aura each day for 'holes'. If you find any, repair them by visualising them being re-woven. There are many healing deities to work with: Apollo, Archangel Raphael (beloved of New Agers) and the Irish Goddess, Brigid.
- Maintain, or aim for, perfect health. Stay strong, fit, and sleep well.
- Do not drink alcohol or take drugs (unless they are absolutely necessary for your survival) during a time of psychic attack. Drugs and alcohol weaken your own energetic field, creating weak spots and holes, and give the attack an entry point.
- Use humming/white noise/music as a shield.

- DO NOT deflect the energetic attack – you will start a feud.
- GROUND the energy instead. Stop the cycle, don't perpetuate it.

Rose and Aleister Crowley wound their way back to Britain via Paris and made their home at Boleskin, an eighteenth-century manor on the edge of Loch Ness, over the ruins of a tenth-century Kirk (church). Together, they awaited the birth of their first child. In late July, a tiny daughter was born at Boleskin, and given the impressive name Nuit Ma Ahathoor Hecate Sappho Jezebel Lilith – or Lilith for short.

Crowley, for a time, was content. In love, with a family, and in a place that he adored, receiving works channeled by spirit, his hunger for every experience seemed to have been replaced by something new to this sensation-drenched man. Fulfillment.

The Strange Laird of Boleskin

When first mentioning Crowley, you can almost certainly expect any listener who has heard of him to recoil. His reputation is undeniably tarnished. Though many of his philosophies are highly dubious in terms of moral integrity – he was not above a certain sadistic tone in many ceremonies, especially during the drug-induced fugues that accompanied the later rituals in Italy – he asked nothing of another he would not do himself, and he was much loved by many … and thoroughly detested by many more. His courage and skill, his intelligence, hard work and creativity cannot be questioned. Crowley was a new man for a new era – an era that had yet to come. He was, in very real terms, ahead of his time. But he managed well enough, buffered against the excesses of his explorations by his money, his intellect and his athletic prowess. He had courage, and was an explorer, and he was rich – and he was rarely even in the country.

During this time, Crowley felt the way to get to "the light" was through the shadowlands of personality. He certainly explored them well. Was he a diabolist? A Witch? A Wizard?

No-one has ever really been able to categorise Crowley, though nearly every authority on the occult has tried. He inspired love, and contempt, loyalty and disgust, friendship, love and fierce condemnation.

Though he was feared, he was also admired by many literary and artistic luminaries of the day – W. Somerset Maugham based his novel *The Magician* on his exploits – savagely exploiting Crowley, whose reputation in London was growing. In some ways, Crowley hated Maugham for this caricature – but in other ways, fame was a drug, and

Crowley loved his drugs. Crowley accused Maugham of plagiarism. Maugham responded in kind:

'Though Aleister Crowley served, as I have said, as the model for Oliver Haddo, it is by no means a portrait of him. I made my character more striking in appearance, more sinister and more ruthless than Crowley. I gave him magical powers that Crowley, though he claimed them, certainly never possessed.'

Such disrespect disturbed Crowley, and kept him in London, determined to salvage his reputation. Gradually, Boleskin was visited less and less often. Rose began to drink when she realised her husband was more intent than ever on experiencing all of life, including other lovers, men and women, and they fought as they travelled to the east. When they were in the UK, he left Boleskin for months at a time, and began collecting about him in London societies of lost souls, talented artists, beautiful women, beautiful men. After a fight in Egypt in 1906, Rose took Lilith back to Britain – but Lilith never made it, dying in Rangoon on the way. Crowley blamed Rose, and even though they went on to have another daughter, their relationship was unable to withstand the pressure. Crowley buried himself in the occult, deciding to create a new mystical order, the A∴A∴, which borrowed heavily from the Golden Dawn. Crowley's *Book of the Law* was complete – in essence, Thelema, the religion of pure will, was born. In 1909, the strain between Rose and Crowley led to their divorce, but Rose remained at Boleskin for years until she was finally institutionalised for alcoholism.

A Star is Born

Re-enter Leila Waddell from the beginning of our journey through Crowley's life. The two met in 1910 and fell deeply in love. Waddell joined Crowley as his muse and they entertained London's elite with re-enacted rites of Artemis and Eleusis in exclusive theaters.

For a time they were the darlings of the creative set, equally despised, adored and feted. There was another motive behind the theatrical performances – Crowley's inheritance was running out, and for the first time he was in danger of not being able to do exactly what he wanted to do. So he became a spy again. As a British double agent, his role was to infiltrate the pro-German movement in New York, feed back information regarding its leaders, and simultaneously make it look foolish. He did this with characteristic gusto. He agitated in New York and Washington, ripped up his British passport to cause a scandal, wrote for *Vanity Fair*, cast horoscopes, and lived in cheap boarding houses from Greenwich Village to New Orleans. In his own time, he continued with his rites and works, adding all the time to *The Equinox*, a magazine that was the voice of the Thelemic order.

When he returned to England he was near destitute, relying on donations from admirers, and homeless, having had to sell Boleskin to pay creditors. He was attacked in the press, called a traitor, and in this atmosphere of hostility and poverty his health suffered. Crowley began to have severe asthma attacks, and a doctor prescribed a common drug of the day to overcome his condition – heroin. Crowley soon developed an addiction that consumed what was left of his money and whatever rags of reputation that remained.

He moved. He went to Paris and took up with two new scarlet women, one of whom had his child. He began to dream of a community of Thelemites, living in peace and isolation, where he could write, experiment, make love, take heroin, do yoga, undertake rites, paint without interference or condemnation. And somehow he managed to scrape together what was needed to take him and his small band of loyal lovers, friends and followers to an abandoned villa in Italy. It was a time of squalor, depravity, decadence and madness. Film stars, Thelemites and intellectuals visited. Some stayed for years, others for days. One young man died after self-harming and drinking from a polluted stream. And stories were filtering back to London about perversion, sex Magick, neglected children, torture;

and Crowley was becoming a mythical figure. Italy could not cope with this and Crowley and his companions in the madness that the Abbey had become were deported.

There is so much more to this story. But the truth is, at this time, Crowley had to work – to write for money, to try and beat heroin. He had lost his money, his incredible health, his looks, but his intellect and charisma were intact. He managed in his later years to make good friends, create great works, connect with writers and spies, like Ian Fleming, with whom he corresponded, and be, somehow, greatly loved, despite everything he did to make people hate him.

One of his greatest friends in those years was Lady Frieda Harris, the wife of a prominent politician and a talented painter. They were not lovers – true friends, they worked on what was to become one of Crowley's most enduring contributions to Magickal work, the Thoth Tarot deck. Despite its completion, he never lived to see it published. To this day, it is recognised as one of the greatest of Tarot projects, a masterful, Magickal deck, poetic, sexual, powerful.

Crowley in his later years met Gerald Gardner, an anthropologist who claimed to have been initiated by a group of Witches who could trace their lineage back to the sixteenth century. Fascinated with Crowley, Gardner asked him to contribute to the rituals he was writing for a path he was re-weaving from the fragments of the Old Ways, Witchcraft, which he would go on to call Wicca.

The year 1947 was a year of highs and lows – one of his closest friends, Jack Parsons, taught some of the secret rites to L. Ron Hubbard, and undertook the Babalon Working with the future father of Scientology. Crowley was horrified. 'I get fairly frantic,' wrote Crowley, 'when I contemplate the idiocy of these louts.'

The Beatles and the Beast

It was John Lennon who insisted that Crowley's face be included on the cover for *Sgt. Pepper's Lonely Hearts Club Band*.

'The whole Beatle idea was to do what you want, right? To take your own responsibility,' Lennon said, during an interview.

Lennon's quotes from 1966, on The Beatles being bigger than Jesus, and about Christianity nearing its end times, had caused a huge uproar. To this day, conspiracy theorists believe that *Sgt. Pepper's* is dedicated to Aleister Crowley – others believe that Paul McCartney died after the making of this album in a ritual sacrifice and Crowley re-incarnated through Paul's dead body, replacing him in The Beatles, living still as a rockstar. It is hard to say what is true and what is not, but there seems nothing less likely to be a delusion than these claims. What is true is that Lennon read

The Book of the Law and found resonance with some of what Crowley believed. Thelema – or the religion of pure Will – had found a place within the mind of the most avante garde member of The Beatles.

The Man Who Died From Living Too Much

Despite these bursts of creative and critical energy, Crowley was dying. He had rooms at a boarding house in Hastings, called Netherwood, paid for by Lady Frieda Harris, who had also hired a nurse to care for him. He passed away peacefully, a lover and a son by his side.

Frieda Harris wept when she received the telegram, writing, 'I will miss him greatly.' Friends paid tribute, and newspapers rejoiced at the death of the world's supposed most evil man.

It was even said that, at the moment of his death, a great peal of thunder tore across the sky. Theatrical as that was, the old magician still had one more trick up his sleeve.

On the 5th of December, a motley group of bohemians, artists, scientists and mystics gathered at Brighton cemetery. Out loud was read the scandalous 'Hymn To Pan', sections from the Gnostic Mass were recited, and finally, parts of the *Book of the Law*, Crowley's major Magickal work, rang defiantly across the Christian cemetery. Outraged neighbours made indignant protests to Brighton council, and the Beast's ashes were quietly taken away and eventually buried in the United States, beneath a tree.

Led Zeppelin and the Laird of Boleskin

Aleister Crowley's Loch Ness home, Boleskin, is now on any dedicated occult tourist's bucket list. In its time it has said to be cursed, the site of demons unleashed during an incomplete ritual, the execution site for a previous laird, and a home for the faerie people of the Highlands, who are not considered to be benevolent Tinkerbells.

Purchased in 1970 by Led Zeppelin's Jimmy Page, a dedicated Crowley aficionado, Page's childhood friend Malcolm Dent became its caretaker for the duration of Page's occupation of the Beast's old lair.

'Doors would be slamming all night, you'd go into a room and carpets and rugs would be piled up,' Malcolm said. 'We just used to say that was Aleister doing his thing.'

'Strange things have happened in that house which have nothing to do with Crowley. The bad vibes were already there,' Page said about Boleskin.

Though he was undoubtedly bordering on insane at times, and his motives were almost always egocentric, Crowley was a force of nature, and one which tore apart the stiffness and prudity of Victorian society. He had a tremendous ability to assert his will, create havoc, incite great love and fierce hatred. He was prolific, creative, wild, and some say a genius. He created works that sell more today than ever before, and he and Lady Frieda's Thoth Tarot is one of the most powerful decks that exists. He took drugs, he experimented, he could be cruel, and kind and very generous. He was athletic, courageous, loyal and disgusting – an acid-tongued mystic, the Oscar Wilde of the Occult. He was a human paradox, and he is celebrated in rock music in lyrics by David Bowie, Ozzy Osborne, The Police, Ministry and the Manic Street Preachers. A new generation of boy bands, hip-hop stars and rappers have discovered him. Jay-Z wears shirts emblazoned with his words, Do What Thou Wilt, and the Jonas Brothers borrow his rebellious cool when they wear T-shirts with his face plastered over them. He is mythic, he is undying, and he was recently voted one of the Greatest British men who ever lived.

Who knows what the future will make of Aleister Crowley? For it seems, as a man ahead of his times, that he is somehow now more relevant than he ever was before.

Perhaps, after all, his Magick has made him immortal.

The Children of the Revolution

❦

BRITAIN, 1929. The island of Merlin between the two great wars was a land on the verge of a spiritual revolution – but one very special little girl didn't know that yet. Doreen was seven years old, but she had already felt the magic pour into her as she gazed enraptured at the moon, its glorious fullness hypnotising her at night. Staring out through a dirty London window, she sensed that there was what was seen, and what was unseen, and that the unseen was what she was most interested in. Something lay behind the power she felt when she looked at the moon. Something lay behind people and how they behaved, and what they said. Something bigger than her, bigger too than the Church her family held so dear. She didn't know what it was – she only knew that it was there.

She went with her mother and father to the service every Sunday, but a part of her felt utterly separate to the prayers and the rituals and the church in South London they attended. Instead, Doreen whispered secrets to the moon, danced when no-one was watching, wondered if there was a Goddess as well as a God, and wished with all her young heart that she had been born in more ancient times, so she could be herself.

At thirteen, she discovered that her mother, a housekeeper, was being bullied by her employers. One thing Doreen could not abide was cruelty – and so she decided she would help her mother using the power she knew lay behind everything she could see, the power she could feel when she gazed at the moon.

Without being taught, and just by following her intuition, Doreen gathered three strands of the bullies' hair and a little clay. From these she fashioned a little dolly. She took the dolly outside under the moon, and wrapped the strands once, twice, three times about the mouth of the doll. She whispered to the moon to please help her mother, to silence the cruel words of her tormentor.

But when her mother found Doreen holding the little clay doll and telling it to stay away from her family, she was terrified for her daughter. And so, on the cusp of adolescence, Doreen found herself sent straight to her own personal hell – a convent school.

Doreen loved aspects of the life – the rituals, the chants, even the women who were strong – but the beatings and the fear lost them her respect. She felt scornful of their lack

of love and
their belief
that women
were inferior.
She knew she
was not evil,
or lesser. How
could she be,
when the rapture
of being alive
filled her again
and again? Her
nature thrilled
to the moon,
the change of
seasons, to the
sight of deer

and blackbird and bud and flower. At fifteen, after being told
of Eve's sinful nature, and of women's unclean bodies, she
gathered her diaries full of spells she was working on, and left
the convent forever.

Doreen began to teach herself – she read Aleister Crowley,
his *Book of the Law*, the Gnostic Mass, moved on to Margaret
Murray, the famous female sociologist who claimed that
Witches were woman who had ruled society for thousands of
years. She taught herself to type, and at nineteen she found
a job in South Wales. There she met a sailor, and, caught in

the romantic pressure cooker war brings to all new couples, she married, but he was declared missing in action, presumed deceased within six months of their union. In London, grieving, she met and married her second husband, a handsome Spaniard fighting for the French Resistance who was healing from his injuries in the capital. His name was Casimero Valiente, and thus her name became Doreen Valiente, and would remain so for the rest of her long and wonderful life.

~~

The Mother of Witchcraft

Doreen Valiente is perhaps the great Mother of modern Witchcraft, a woman whose deeply poetic rituals and intelligent, calm demeanor endeared her to thousands of spiritual explorers. In 1951, something wonderful happened – the Witchcraft Laws were repealed in Britain, and suddenly people who were fascinated by the tattered remnants of the old Magick, folk who had managed to hang on to life throughout Western Europe, were able to connect with a pagan past without fear of prosecution.

It was around this time that Doreen Valiente picked up her local paper and read an article about a man called Gerald Gardner, who was involved with a Witchcraft museum on the Isle of Man. Doreen wrote to Gerald

Gardner, and the pair struck up a friendship, which led to a meeting, and ultimately to Doreen's initiation into what Gerald called Wicca – the reconstructed practices of a group of hereditary Witches who lived in the New Forest, and who had been instrumental in the Magickal acts protecting Britain during World War II. Doreen's Magickal name became Ameth – Hebrew for 'truth'.

Described with love by all who met her, Doreen was said to be gentle, intelligent, learned, calm, unassuming, and artistic. And she went on to rework Gardner's Wiccan rituals, which she recognised had pilfered large passages from Crowley's works, and from various forms of Freemasonry. The Charge of the Goddess, an inspiring piece of ritual poetry, was re-crafted by Valiente, and the Wiccan rede, too, owes much to her rewriting and intelligent revisions.

The Last Witch of Britain

The contrast between the spiritually open England of 1951, the year of Doreen's initiation, and the repressive England of eight years earlier could not be more pronounced. In 1943, the mother and father of a young sailor went to see a medium, Helen Duncan, who held a séance for the parents, along with other people eager to know the fate of their loved ones in the afterlife. During the session, Helen Duncan brought through a spirit – the spirit of a young sailor. He said he had gone down on the HMS *Barham*.

The parents recognized his name, his description, his words. They were devastated, but puzzled, as the Barham had not been declared lost at sea, and they had thought their son might still be alive and well. The parents' search for answers led the police to Helen Duncan's door, and she was arrested under the Witchcraft Act, and in 1944 was sent to prison, where she stayed for nine months.

Why was Helen Duncan targeted? Because the Barham had gone down months before her séance – but the government had not yet announced its loss. How, they demanded, had she known about its sinking by the enemy? They questioned Duncan brutally, insisting that she was a German spy, refusing to believe her explanation that she spoke to the dead, and so she was imprisoned – the last person in England to be imprisoned under the Witchcraft Act. Eight years later the Witchcraft Act was repealed, and in Britain at least, Witches, Wizards and mediums, card readers and intuitives could begin to go about their business without fear of being prosecuted under an Act that had last been modified in 1735.

The Magickal Battle of Britain

While Helen Duncan was suffering for her psychic talents, a small but powerful band of spiritualists and occultists were growing increasingly concerned at the use by the Nazis of occult science. The use of symbols, and a perversion of the Nordic Magickal path were being used by the SS, and this use of Magick was giving, Britain's Witches and Wizards felt, the Nazis a clear advantage in the war. The mystical revolution of the nineteenth and twentieth centuries had created a band of spiritual warriors, patriots who were determined to fight fire with fire – Magick with Magick – in a series of meditations, rites and spellcraftings that were intended to support the army, the air force, the navy, in a special brand of energetic warfare that would keep Britain – the home of Merlin – free.

On July 31, 1940, members of diverse mystical groups and covens, including Gerald Gardner's traditional Witches of the New Forest, travelled to the south of England to a secret location to raise a 'cone of power' over all of Britain. The participants were many, and even more joined in at a distance, united by a series of letters detailing the time, the ritual, and the focus for their ritual. It is said that the energy raised was so strong that five people died soon afterwards, their life-force depleted by all they had given.

The respected mystic and influential occultist Dion Fortune was the person responsible for the letters. Week after week she had posted them out, readying the psychic troops, building up their Magickal skills in readiness for what would become the legendary Magickal Battle of Britain. Her meditations were based on the rituals of the

Golden Dawn, and part of the evocation was a call to Merlin and to King Arthur – the visualisations included Arthur's sword rising from within the Tor of Glastonbury.

A second ritual took place on January 22, 1941, led by one of Aleister Crowley's closest friends and former pupils, William Seabrook, and was attended by mystics, an heiress, intellectuals and soldiers. During this ritual, a powerful curse was laid upon Hitler – and we still have the words today:

'Hitler! You are the enemy of man and of the world; therefore we curse you. We curse you by every tear and drop of blood you have caused to flow. We curse you with the curses of all who have cursed you!'

And while Britain was bombed and blasted, night after night, the planned invasion never took place, perhaps in part because of these Wizards and Witches who worked in the forests, through the humble power of the post office.

The Wizards Rise Again: The Druid, the Witch and the Nudist Camp

After the war, the world had changed. Amidst this soup of social change, two men met and became friends at a nudist camp in Hertfordshire in 1950. The young, studious and shy history buff, Ross Nichols, encountered the wizened, flamboyant and extroverted anthropologist Gerald Gardner.

He had, he told Nichols, been initiated into Witchcraft
by old Dorothy Clutterbuck of the New Forest Witches,
who had been part of the great, psychic Battle of Britain,
and he was, he said, going to revive the ancient witch-cult
of Britain. He would call this Wicca, based on *wicce* – an
Anglo-Saxon word with many meanings, including 'wise',
and 'to bend and to shape'.

Nichols would go on to edit Gardner's ground-breaking
book, *Witchcraft Today*, before creating the Order of Bards,
Ovates and Druids – a poetic reanimation of the ancient
order of British Druids, linking modern Druidry to the
Merlins, the Wizards of ancient times. OBOD is now
the largest worldwide Druidic organisation in the world.
Gardner's Wicca would develop many variations as the
century matured. The Wizard and the Witch would remain
friends, but their paths diverged – one quietly writing
poetry and ecstatically exploring Druidry, the other courting
publicity, which drew to him the High Priestess Doreen
Valiente and a vast number of initiates. Both would leave
enduring legacies. On October 1, 2010, Druidry was finally
recognised as a religion within the United Kingdom. In
April 2015, Deborah Maynard, a Wiccan, was invited by a
Senator to address the Iowa House of Representatives, and
lead the opening prayers – a moment that signaled that even
in conservative middle America, Gardner's Witchcraft had
become respectable.

Satan Goes to the Movies – Anton LaVey and the Hollywood Connection

While Witches and Wizards and Druids and Wise Women are now being embraced by the mainstream, the belief that there is a connection between Witchcraft and Wizardry and the Devil lingers. There is perhaps one very influential man whose ability to harness scandal and seduce the famous is the reason these accusations endure.

In 1966, in a San Francisco on the verge of being the Flower Children capital of the world, a small group of lost souls gathered every Friday night. Led by Anton LaVey, a former carnival roustabout, police photographer and musician, they listened, enraptured, to LaVey's impassioned sermons, and joined in daring discussions on the occult. Numbers swelled, drawn by LaVey's hypnotic personality, startling looks and amazing stories. Within months the first Church of Satan was formed. LaVey knew exactly how sensational the name was – and its brazen outrageousness attracted well-known rebel artists and counter culture leaders. With his shaven head, dark robes and piercing eyes, LaVey soon had a growing Church of Satan – and a sophisticated philosophy of personal freedom from the government, and conditioning, to go along with the shocking name. Its infamy reached new heights when, in late 1966, blonde bombshell and Hollywood sex symbol Jayne Mansfield declared she wanted to meet LaVey. Mansfield, a star whose box office bankability was in decline, needed a career boost. She had long been fascinated by the occult, and was also searching for ways to help heal her son, who had suffered devastating meningitis.

'Mr LaVey took me into another room to show me the black-magic charms from the Devil, and he presented me with one,' she told one newspaper. 'He said I was now the High Priestess of his Church.' Mansfield wore her talisman, a black and pink inverted pentacle symbol, enjoying the fresh flush of notoriety.

LaVey and Mansfield began a wild affair that would scandalise Hollywood and ensure LaVey suddenly had a nationwide mainstream cachet. Hollywood lawyer Sam Brody was Mansfield's lover and manager at the time and he and LaVey fought over the fading star, their hatred escalating with their sexual rivalry.

'Sam Brody,' LaVey told one reporter in the 1990s, 'worked overtime at being detestable, kept her doped and liquored up and had guys fooling around with her in the bedroom while he took pictures. If she ever left him, he promised to ruin her career and see that she lost custody of her kids. He was despicable, utterly despicable!'

Brody was furious about LaVey using Mansfield to raise his profile, and the pair fought viciously, Brody calling LaVey a charlatan, LaVey firing back that Brody was a pimp and a pervert. 'I told him that I had more power than he could possibly imagine. I told him that he would be dead within a year,' LaVey said.

Two weeks after the vicious showdown, Brody and Mansfield headed to New Orleans for a burlesque appearance by Jayne, and on June 29, 1967, a semi-trailer collided with the car Brody was driving. Jayne's three children survived the accident, but Brody and Mansfield died instantly – Mansfield, they said, was decapitated. LaVey was distraught: his curse had worked, but it had also taken his lover and benefactor.

Their lurid deaths raised LaVey's profile, and his Satanic Bible went on to sell over one million copies; it has been translated into six languages and reprinted thirty times. His infamy has never died, and when he passed away in 1997, LaVey's funeral was attended by hundreds of musicians, readers, the curious, Church of Satan acolytes, former lovers, and reporters. A lot of reporters.

Although much of LaVey's Church of Satan philosophy resonates with rebellion, also seems inspired by creative and artistic philosophies, it unfortunately reinforced the association between Satanism and Witchcraft, and the inversion of the pentacle as a symbol. It's something many Wiccans, Witches and modern-day Wizards wish they did not have to deal with nearly every day.

The Bohemian Witch of Kings Cross

When the 1960s hit, they hit with such power that the world was changed forever. Disillusioned with governments and war, economics and taxes, restrictions and sexism, young people in the Western world began to rebel. In Australia, the artistic and the rebellious gathered in Kings Cross, the nation's bohemian epicenter. And at the heart of the Cross was the fascinating, talented and scandalous Witch, Rosaleen Norton.

Like Doreen Valiente, Rosaleen began her Magickal explorations young. In 1925, at the age of fourteen, she was thrown out of the Church of England Girls' School in Chatswood, Sydney. The reason? Rosaleen was an extraordinarily talented artist, but her subject matter consisted of werewolves, blood-drinking vampires and spirits rising from cemeteries – her work was labelled depraved, corrupt and likely to disturb the girls. Roie as she called herself, took her portfolio of depravity to East Sydney Technical College and studied under Rayner Hof, who introduced her to pagan themes and nurtured her talent. Rosaleen dived in.

To fund her art, Rosaleen 'busked' as an artist, creating pavement art in the city during the day and working in nightclubs as a waitress in the evenings. She even worked for a time as a cadet journalist.

She married in 1940, yet never took her husband's name, and her work began to appear in magazines. In 1949 she

met the poet Gavin Greenlees and they became lovers, and Roie, began to bloom. Greenlees was inspired by Roie, and her work soared after they formed their bohemian alliance. She held an exhibition in 1949 of pagan-themed erotic drawings in Melbourne – and it was this fearless spirit that led to the first raid upon Norton's work. The exhibition was ambushed by the police, who took the paintings titled 'Lucifer', 'Witches Sabbath' and 'Individuation', and Roie was charged with obscenity.

The court case became a sensation, but the Witch of Kings Cross unapologetically held her ground, explaining the occult symbolism behind her work, so impressing the magistrate with her intellect and eloquence that the case was dismissed. But the notoriety stuck.

Her creative collaboration with Greenlees, a book titled *The Art of Rosaleen Norton*, was released in 1952, but the police tipped off the censors and her publisher was charged with producing an obscene publication. They sent copies to the United States, to avoid Australia's condemnation, but the book was burned by customs officials when it arrived. Instead of earning royalties and creating art, Greenlees and Norton spent their time dealing with police raids, and moving from tiny flat to even tinier flat, making their living however they could.

But one person who had read Roie's book was the celebrated English conductor, Sir Eugene Goosens, who fell under the spell of her art. When he arrived in Australia to conduct the Sydney Symphony Orchestra, he arranged a meeting with Roie, and the impoverished Australian occult artist and the Knight of the Realm became lovers, engaging in sex Magick, leading naked rites to the Old Gods, exploring trance meditation and downing LSD. With Goosens' patronage and sincere ardour came the cream of the artistic elite, and more and more people began to gather in Rosaleen's tiny Kings Cross apartment for the Rites to Pan. Greenlees remained loyal, Goosens was besotted, paintings were selling to socialites, but Roie was arrested again for obscenity. Each time she went before the court she was witty, serious, intellectual and fearless, seemingly unfazed by the ongoing persecution. The newspapers adored the story, and her reputation as the Witch of Kings Cross was cemented. But for Goosens, his adoration of his Magickal mistress meant his reputation and his career as a conductor were in great danger.

Goosens returned to London to be dubbed a Knight of the Realm, and while he was gone, the Australian police set up an elaborate sting. When Sir Goosens flew into Mascot airport to return to Roie and to the Opera House, he was intercepted by customs officials, reporters and photographers from *The Sun* newspaper, as well as over five policemen. They went through his luggage, unearthing incense, a rubber mask, and erotic art – a gift for Roie. It was enough. The

Knight was charged and convicted of violating the Customs Act, and deported. The British tabloids took hold of the story. He left Australia a broken man, and returned to England ruined.

Roie remained poor her whole life, but her paintings now sell for a small fortune. In 1982 *The Art of Rosaleen Norton* was republished, and sells well today. Roie painted until her death in the Sacred Heart Hospice in Darlinghurst in 1979 from an aggressive form of cancer. She never recanted her paganism, and she has since become a darling of the bohemian, the artistic, and a modern pagan heroine.

The Age of Sisterhood

As the counterculture movement gathered momentum, the seventies gave birth to Feminism – and simultaneously, this led to the discovery of the Witch as a feminist icon, the Wizard as her adoring accomplice. Reclaiming the word Witch became a point of honour, and feminists declared themselves the daughters of the Witches they could not burn. Zsunanna B. Budapest. Starhawk. Phyllis Curott. Dianic Witchcraft, focussing exclusively on the Goddess, began to flourish, and Wizard and Witch lovers and collaborators Oberon Zell Ravenheart and Morning Glory began to shift the direction in which modern Magickal practice was heading.

The Crooked Path to Pendle Hill

In 2012, four hundred people walked the cold miles to
the tall hill outside a little village called Pendle in
England's north. Each was dressed in black and carried
a broom, their heads bent under the weight of their tall
pointed hats. When they arrived at the wind-blasted tip
of the peak, the Poet Laureate of England read a moving
poem. The date 1612 was carved into the hillside
100 metres high. Voices shook, and tears were shed.
The reason? The 400th anniversary of the Pendle Witch
Trials. And for the first time in four centuries a whole town
was in mourning for the people who'd lost their lives so
many years before.

Hundreds of visitors attempted to climb the hill to leave
flowers and offerings, so many that the council imposed a
curfew to prevent people getting lost on the frosty slopes of
Pendle Hill.

The people who had come to their end at the hill four-
hundred years earlier would have been astounded to know
their fate meant anything at all to people so far in the
future – their lives had meant little enough to the people
of their own time.

In 1612, beneath the hill, on a path leading from the
village to the town, a peddler, John Law, was travelling on
the road and passed a young woman named Alizon Devize.

The Devizes were a clan of cunning-men and women – folk
Magicians, midwives and herbalists, who offered ill-wishes
and blessings, charms and potions in exchange for a fee.
John Law did not know this, so when Alizon Devize asked
him to sell her a pin, he brushed off the woman in rags,
thinking her offer to pay for a pin was a joke.

The Devizes were proud folk, skilled and fierce, and
Alizon repeated her wish to buy some pins. The peddler
mocked her garments, asking her why he should bother
unpacking his goods for a dirty beggar like her? Alizon's
eyes flashed, and a curse spilled from her lips as the peddler
passed her on the ancient road. Within minutes, John Law
fell to the ground, paralysed down one side. He had suffered
a stroke – known as elf-shot or elf-struck in the old times –
and his son went straight to the local Justice of the Peace to
accuse Alizon Devize of Witchcraft.

Within four weeks, nearly all the members of the Devize
family were in prison. One by one they were questioned, and
put to the question – tortured. Alizon begged forgiveness
for the ill-wish that had fallen from her lips. And somehow,
during the pain of the torture, a rival clan of cunning-folk
were brought into the trial. Alizon demanded to know what
the court would do with Anne Whittle and Anne Redferne
– they had, she proclaimed, outraged, murdered four men.
Why should she be tortured for ill-wishing, why should
her grandmother be in irons when others who had done

worse were free? So, Anne Redferne, Anne Whittle, Alizon Devize and her eighty-year-old grandmother Elizabeth, the undisputed Wise Woman of Pendle, were sent to Lancaster to face trial.

Desperate to help his grandmother and sister, James Devize gathered sympathisers together in the forest of Pendle. The Justice of the Peace heard of the gathering and arrested fourteen more people.

Within the next month Alizon, Anne Whittle and Anne Redferne were hung, along with six villagers who had gone to the forest to support them. Elizabeth Devize died in prison, old and sick and starved to death. Another woman who had gone to the forest, Janet Preston, was tried and sent to the gallows in York.

The hangings had great impact – held by the Justice of the Peace to curry favour with King James I, the courts found the accused guilty of sexual acts with the Devil, of demonic possession and of holding gatherings to worship their master, Satan.

None of which was true.

❧

Today in Pendle you can take tours in buses painted with images of Witches. Signs featuring Witches flying on broomsticks point the way to the hill, and on that hill lies a stone, which locals circle three times to bring good luck –

and to catch a glimpse of the ghosts of the Witches. And the events of 2012, and the sincere respect and sadness the people of Pendle expressed, show that something very deep has changed within us.

Somehow, we have come to a place where we are beginning to accept that there are those people who want to learn what lies beyond the evidence of their eyes. That there are people who want to understand the ways in which the world works, and will use Magick to investigate and more deeply understand all that is about them.

How Many Witches and Wizards Are There Today?

It's impossible to count people who want to stay quiet about their beliefs: old habits die hard, and many Witches and Wizards still want to stay within the broom closet. It feels safer there.

But what we do know is that the official numbers are growing. Take, for example, the numbers of Wiccans within the US armed forces. According to 2005 defense department statistics, there were more than 1800 active duty soldiers identifying as Wiccans. In 2007 the *Washington Post* published data from the Pentagon files – numbering 1511 Wiccans in the air force and 354 marines as practitioners. At least 4000 people in uniform identified as Witches and Wiccans. How does this translate to the mainstream population? In the United States, there are likely to be over one million practising pagans. In Britain it is thought that there are over 250,000 people who are practising an old, indigenous religion – identifying as Witches, Wizards, pagans and Wiccans. Professor Ronald Hutton, an authority on Witchcraft, estimates that the numbers growing each year.

In the 2006 Australian census 30,000 people declared they were pagan. Just as it is throughout the world, this number is likely to be hugely inaccurate due to the countless people who are not ready to be open about their practice and their faith.

Turning the Wheel of the Year

I<small>F YOU</small> would like to explore the workings of Witches and Wizards, you may like to celebrate some of the festivals of the Wheel of the Year. There are eight festivals – four are seasonal, four are astronomical – and each speaks to our souls of change, maturation, death, birth, growth and balance. The dates for the festivals depend on which hemisphere you are in – see following to discover the best dates for you to tune in to these Magickal times, and work your own personal brand of Witchcraft and Wizardry.

To begin, consider setting up an altar – it can be simple and small – use the table of correspondences in the following pages to decide what you would like to decorate your sacred space with, and to explore the deities and trees to begin to grow your own knowledge and practice of these ancients arts.

Blessed be!

Samhain

A festival held to honour the beginning of the Dark Times. Ancestor worship, endings and justice are its themes.

Southern Hemisphere: April 30–May 1
Northern Hemisphere: October 31–November 1

Names
Samhain
Oidhche Shamhna
Feile na Marbh
Halloween
Day of the Dead
All Soul's Eve

Deities
Hecate
Lilith
Cerridwen
Morrigan
Kali
Cailleach (Kah-lee)
The Crone

Animals
Owl
Cat
Pig
Hawk
Eagle

Stones
Jet
Obsidian
Onyx
Smokey quartz
Spirit (fairy) quartz

Plants
Apples
Corn
Mistletoe
Evergreen

Herbs
Rosemary
Sage
Mugwort
Allspice
Nightshade

Winter Solstice

A time when Witches and Wizards honoured the greatest darkness, and prayed for the birth of the baby Sun God, and the return of the Light and warmth and Life.
Southern Hemisphere: June 21–23
Northern Hemisphere: December 21–23

Names
Yule
Wassail
Festival of Dionysus
Festival of Mithras

Deities
Odin
Freya
Skahdi
Isis
Demeter
Dagda

Animals
Robin
Wren
Boar

Stones
Ruby
Bloodstone
Carnelion
Citrine
Garnet

Plants
Yew
Laurel

Birch
Cranberries
Pine tree – to make the yule tree!
Mistletoe
Cedar
Nuts

Herbs
Sage
Bayberry

Imbolc

Witches and Wizards once celebrated this festival with the
lighting of candles and fires to tempt the sun to come closer
to us once again. It became entwined with the worship of
the Irish Goddess Brigid.
Southern Hemisphere: August 1–2
Northern Hemisphere: February 1–2

Names
Imbolc
Feast of Bride
Brigid's day
Blessing of Bride
Candlemas
Groundhog day
Festival of Lights

Deities
Bride
Brigid
All deities that honour the youthful feminine

Animals
Swan
Ewes
Cows
All birthing animals
All lactating animals
All baby animals

Stones
Clear quartz
Yellow tourmaline
Rose quartz
Hematite
Pearls

Plants
Ash
Oak
Rowan
Reeds

Herbs
Angelica
Basil

Bay
Benzoin
Red herb
Dandelion
Dill

Spring Equinox

Witches and Wizards honoured the Goddess Ostara, whose symbols are eggs and hares. She was said to dwell in the moon, and to draw closer at this time and send blessings of fertility and growth to the land.

Names
Ostara
Alban Eiler
The day of trees Oestre
Lady Day
Gwyl Canol Gwenwynol

Deities
Ostara
Blodeuwedd
Rhiannon

Stones
Moonstone
Aquamarine

Rose quartz
Moss agate
Green moonstone

Animals
The Hare
Rabbits
The chicken, duck, goose – all birds – for their sacred eggs!

Plants
All bulbs
Jasmine
Daffodils
Narcissus
Anything that flowers/grows in your region at Spring
Anemone
Violets
Roses
Lily

Herbs (and resins)
Sage
Frankincense
Myrrh

Beltane

This is the festival of fertility, to urge crops to grow, for the animals to mate, for the lovers to unite in ceremonies led by

Witches and Wizards and leap over the Beltane fires together.
Maypoles, symbolising masculine power, were danced
around, and flower crowns were worn by young women.
Southern Hemisphere: October 31–November 1
Northern Hemisphere: April 30–May 1

Names
Beltane
Beltaine
May Day
Celtic Flower Festival
Walpurgis night
Cetsamhain

Deities
Bel
Cernunnos
Grianne
Flora
The Green Man
Sulis
Sheela na Gig
Rhiannon

Animals
Stag
Deer

Honey bees

Lambs

Calves

Stones

Ruby

Garnet

Citrine

Clear quartz

Amber

Topaz

Sunstone

Malachite

Orange calcite

Plants

Birch

Oak

Ash

Thorn

Rowan

Apple

Alder

Maple

Elm

Gorse

Holly

Hawthorn

Herbs
All seeds – anything that can grow (symbolising fertility)
Strawberries
Raspberries
Peaches
Apple
Vanilla
Cinnamon
Mead (made with herbs)
Wild roses

Summer Solstice

This is a time when Witches and Wizards celebrate the longest day, to feast with friends and family, and to connect with the faeries, to whom this day is dedicated. Think Shakespeare's *A Midsummer's Night's Dream*, his play set on the night before solstice, a play about love, sexuality, enchantment and romance.

Southern Hemisphere: December 21–23
Northern Hemisphere: June 21–23

Names
Litha
Feast of the Faery
Alban Hefin
Midsummer Eve
Althing

Deities
Aine – Irish Faery Queen
The Green Man
Dana
Gwydion
Llew
Cerridwen
Morgan le Fay

Stones
Amethyst
Malachite
Golden topaz
Opal
Lapis lazuli
Quartz
Azurite

Animals
Horse
Hawk
Badger
Bilby
Snake

Plants
Apple
Grapevine

Passionfruit
Hawthorn
Beech
Orange tree
Lemon tree

Herbs
Thyme
Honeysuckle
Lemon verbena
Lemon vervain
Lavender
Daisy

Lughnasad

Lughnasad is dedicated to the Celtic God Lugh, to justice
and to light. It is traditional at this time to bring in the
first harvest – symbolically, Witches and Wizards would
give thanks for their personal successes, abundance and
community achievements.
Southern Hemisphere: February 1–2
Northern Hemisphere: August 1–2

Names
Lughnasadh
Harvest

Lammas
Harvest Mother's Day

Deities
Llugh
Llew
Tailtiu – Irish Goddess of the land
The Green Man
The Corn Mother
Demeter
Cerridwen

Animals
Roosters
Calves
Sows
Geese

Stones
Aventurine
Peridot
Sardonyx
Golden tiger's eye
Golden topaz
Ametrine

Plants
Grains – barley, for example
Corn
Blackberry
Mulberry
Oak
Sunflower
Aloes
Oak Leaves

Herbs
Sandalwood
Heather
Acacia
Cyclamen
Fenugreek

Conclusion

Farewell, for now …

I hope you've been thrilled, inspired and perhaps a little outraged by the stories within *Witches and Wizards*. I do trust you have been amazed and inspired by the extraordinary lives of the Magickal folk within its pages. I've loved sharing their true tales of Magick with you, and if *Witches and Wizards* has whetted an appetite for more knowledge, more wonder and more daring within your own life, I will be a very content Witch.

How could we not be intrigued by these stories? Take just a moment now to think on how very fortunate you and I are. To live in a time when Witches and Wizards are no longer persecuted, not in the same way we were. It is not illegal for you to read this book, and nor will it be burned. You may get some funny looks reading it on the train, but let them look! We are now, more than ever before, partaking in a great renaissance of Magick, enjoying vast freedoms, and I want you to make the most of this incredible time of opportunity.

You have the power to make brave choices, unconventional choices, to be inspired, to travel, to live fully and as fearlessly as you can, to drink from the great cauldron that Life offers up to us, every day.

We are heirs to a great fortune: the treasures of the Witches and the Wizards. How will we use this amazing inheritance? What will we do with our unprecedented freedoms? And how will we take our place amongst them?

These are mysteries. But your life – yes, yours – holds the answers.

Be blessed, friend, as you walk the Magickal path. I look forward to meeting you again and urge you to live fully, and fearlessly, every day.

May you be ever-blessed, friend.

Merry meet, merry part, and merry meet again.

Lucy Cavendish
Blood Moon, 2015

Bibliography

I've read many books over the years which have all contributed to this work, including those on the list below, which makes mention of court transcripts and works of the Church that I've read and gleaned information from, and, most importantly, the words of the people involved.

I would also like to acknowledge the British Museum, the Museum of Wiltshire in Salisbury, and the Museum of Witchcraft in Boscastle, Cornwall.

A Book of Secrets and Key of this World Dr John Dee
A Brief and True Narrative of Some Remarkable Passages Relating to Sundry Persons Afflicted by Witchcraft, at Salem Village Reverend Deodat Lawson
A Brief History of the Druids Peter Berresford Ellis
A Discovery of Witches Matthew Hopkins
A Modest Enquiry into the Nature of Witchcraft John Hale
A Transciption of the Court Records: The Salem Witchcraft Papers edited by Paul Boyer and Stephen Nissenbaum
Aleister Crowley: The Biography Tobias Churton
An ABC of Witchcraft Doreen Valiente
Blood on the Mistletoe Ronald Hutton
Dr Dee: An English Opera Damon Albarn and Rufus Norris

High Magic's Aid Gerald B Gardner

Hollywood Babylon Kenneth Anger

John Dee's Conversations with Angels: Cabala, Alchemy and the End of Nature Deborah E Harkness

Life of Merlin Geoffrey of Monmouth

Perdurabo: The Life of Aleister Crowley Richard Kaczynski

Prophet Priest King: The Poetry of Philip Ross Nichols Ross Nichols

Psychic Self-Defense: The Classic Instruction Manual for Protecting Yourself Against Paranormal Attack Dion Fortune

Secret Agent 666: Aleister Crowley, British Intelligence, and the Occult Richard Spence

Stations of the Cross A documentary featuring Rosaleen Norton

The Affair of the Poisons Anne Somerset

The Art of Rosaleen Norton Rosaleen Norton and Gavin Greenlees

The Arthurian Tradition John Matthews

The Equinox Aleister Crowley

The Great Cat Massacre Robert Darnton

The Hieroglyphic Monad Dr John Dee

The History of the Kings of Britain Geoffrey of Monmouth

The Last Witch of Langenburg Thomas Robisheaux

The Magick of Aleister Crowley: A Handbook of the Rituals of Thelema Lon Milo DuQuette

The Magickal Battle of Britain Dion Fortune

The Malleus Maleficarum Heinrich Kramer

The Prophecies of Merlin Geoffrey of Monmouth

The Satanic Bible Anton LaVey

The Stations of the Sun Ronald Hutton

The Training & Work of an Initiate Dion Fortune

The Triumph of the Moon Ronald Hutton

The Way of Wyrd Brian Bates

The Witch of Kings Cross Neville Drury

The Wonders of the Invisible World: Being an Account of Several Witches Lately Executed in New England Cotton Mather

Witchcraft for Tomorrow Doreen Valiente

Witchcraft Today Gerald B Gardner

Witches & Neighbours: The Social and Cultural Context of European Witchcraft Briggs

Women of the Golden Dawn: Rebels and Priestesses: Maud Gonne, Moina Bergson Mathers, Annie Horniman, Florence Farr Mary K Greer

About the Author

Lucy Cavendish is a Witch. She
works Magick every single day of
her life, embracing it as a creed for
personal fulfillment and happiness,
and as a belief system that sees us
as part of Nature, thus giving us all
the motivation to respect, revere and
delight in our unique experience
here on Planet Earth.

Lucy is the author of *Spellbound* (Rockpool Publishing),
The Secret Grimoire of Lucy Cavendish, *The Lost Lands*, *White
Magic*, *Oracle of Shadows and Light*, *Oracle of the Mermaids*,
Oracle of the Shapeshifters, *Wild Wisdom of the Faery
Oracle*, *Oracle of the Dragonfae*, *The Oracle Tarot* and *Magical
Spell Cards*. She has created three CDs featuring Magickal
meditations and offers exciting online courses in the
Magickal arts as well as maintaining a thriving Youtube
station. Her work is published in seven different languages
and has been enjoyed and recommended by Deepak
Chopra and Louise L Hay, but it's the connection with
you – the reader – that she values most of all. Lucy
created *Witchcraft* magazine in 1992, the first magazine of

its kind in the world, and currently writes for Magickal and mainstream magazines around the world. She appears regularly on prime time and alternative television and radio offering insights into the Craft. She is a classic book Witch and adores writing and reading, digging into ancient tomes in the British Museum, live music, hiking, surfing, yoga and creating enchanted workshop experiences. She leads journeys, called Imrammas, to the sacred sites of Ancient Briton, and teaches and travels internationally each year for research. She is a member of the Order of Bards, Ovates and Druids and moves between Sydney, the Sapphire Coast and far northern NSW in Australia.

Visit Lucy's website at: www.lucycavendish.com.au or visit her on her social media sites, which offer everyday ways to connect with her, and with the Magick and wisdom within you.

✳ *Other books by Lucy Cavendish* ✳

Finally a book of spells to empower you!

Spellbound is about connecting you to the magick inside you and activating this transformative power. Come on a mystical journey with Australia's most loved and respected witch, Lucy Cavendish, as she takes you into the secret world of spellcasting. Watch your life become the magickal experience it was always meant to be.

Learn how and why spells work; history of spells; magickal symbols to use in your spells; dressing magickally; rules of spellcasting.

RRP $24.99

ISBN 978-1-925017-15-1

Available at all good bookstores or online at
www.rockpoolpublishing.com.au

MORGAN LE FAY CASTS AWAY THE SCABBARD

THE LEGEND OF SALEM:

"G REV. GEORGE BURROUGHS WAS ACCUSED OF WITCHCRAFT ON THE EVIDENCE OF FEATS OF STR
TRIED, HUNG, AND BURIED BENEATH THE GALLOWS."